Beyond
the Shadows *of*
Memory

Beyond the Shadows of Memory

Navigating Alzheimer's, With Love and Faith

Atiya Saithna

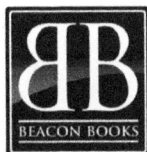

BB
BEACON BOOKS

Published in the UK by Beacon Books and Media Ltd

Earl Business Centre, Dowry Street, Oldham, OL8 2PF, UK.

www.beaconbooks.net

ISBN: 978-1-916955-76-9 Paperback
ISBN: 978-1-916955-77-6 Hardback
ISBN: 978-1-916955-78-3 eBook

Cataloging-in-Publication record for this book is available from the British Library

Cover design by Raees Mahmood Khan

TABLE OF CONTENTS

ACKNOWLEDGEMENTS

I humbly ask Amber, Adnan, Saleem, Gia, Maaryah, Yaseen, and Rayyan—along with our families, friends, and acquaintances—to forgive any shortcomings I may have had along this journey. If I unintentionally caused hurt, I ask for your understanding. This has been a gruelling, exhausting, and overwhelming path—one of the hardest anyone could walk.

I also want to thank the hundreds of people who accompanied me on this journey. Each of you brought a unique perspective that strengthened my soul, even before I fully understood what Alzheimer's truly meant.

Finally, I want to acknowledge Aaliyah Umm Raiyaan's words in *The Power of Du'a*. She reminds us that there is true power in du'a. Believe in it. Use it. Hope in it. Live by it.

I am deeply thankful to my editor, Haneen Shubib from Articulately, for understanding my story so intimately—as if she herself had lived through it.

> *"Anyone who is grateful does so to the profit of his own soul…"*
>
> ....
>
> (Qur'an 31:12)

INTRODUCTION

---◆---

NAVIGATING THE FOG

S ome days feel like I am steering a boat through thick fog. There are no landmarks, no stars to guide me—just a slow, heavy mist pressing in from every side. The sea is quiet, but I feel lost in it. This is what Alzheimer's has done to our life. Not a storm that strikes and passes, but a fog that settles—uninvited, unseen, unrelenting. It wasn't the sudden loss of a loved one, but the slow erosion of a person—the gradual vanishing of the cherished traits that had once made him whole. And with those parts of him, pieces of me felt lost too.

And yet, sometimes the fog lifts, and I see him clearly again.

Qayum was ever so thoughtful. During our early years, he would come home from his bank in Cheapside during lunch just to bask in our shared company. I treasured these thoughtful gestures and made fresh roti to serve with the chicken masala curry I would whip up in under twenty minutes. Sometimes he would say, "I am here just to break the long day for you, to keep you busy preparing lunch for your husband." I felt his genuine care and looked forward to lunch times with him. Those midday pauses were sunlight on the waves—small but steady, warming everything around them.

Much later, despite his Alzheimer's-ravaged mind I was reminded that joy could still reach us in the strangest of moments. I remember one grey February day. We were out walking and passed a tree, drenched and drooping under the relentless drizzle. I remarked on how sorry it looked. Qayum tilted his head slightly and replied with a wry smile, "That tree needs a shower." The twist in his response caught me off guard—turning pity into comedy—and we both laughed heartily. It was the first time in a long while that I saw that glint of playfulness in his eyes—a sparkle through the mist.

There were other moments too—quiet ones, strange ones, deeply human ones. Like the day we visited Harrow shopping centre after a hospital appointment. The rain poured endlessly, our umbrellas flew in all directions, and my hijab clung to my face. I asked, "Why is the bank open at this time?" And Qayum, with a cheeky smile, said, "It's Christmas!"—as if that explained everything. We both laughed in unison. The absurdity of it, the timing, the rain—it all dissolved into that one shared moment. It didn't matter what had just come out of a tormenting neurology appointment in the clinic. In that moment, we were simply two souls laughing in the rain. Despite the seriousness of his condition, his humour always shone through.

But there were also days when the fog thickened without warning—and it frightened me.

A week after sharing our wedding photos, I noticed something shift. He stared at the pictures and didn't recognise himself as the groom. He kept asking, "That's you when you were young?" He made me feel like an alien and refused to accept the woman in the pictures as his wife. I smiled, I explained gently, but inside

I was trembling. What do you do when the man who held your hand through decades no longer sees you? That day, I knew I had entered a part of the sea I did not know how to sail.

Then came the nights—disorienting, fragmented. At 2am, sometimes at 4am, Qayum would be fully dressed, suited and booted, ready to go to the bank. He insisted it was time. I had to explain every time that it was too early. I began sleeping with the keys in my pocket, waking at the slightest sound. These weren't just restless nights. They were nights where I no longer knew which direction the waves would carry us next.

And one evening, before his speech fully faded, he begged me to take him to Pakistan to visit his deceased mother and speak with her about marriage. I reminded him gently that she had passed. Tears rolled down his cheeks. "I miss her so much," he said. I told him he was married now. He looked at me and asked, "To whom?" And I replied, "Me." I wanted to scream it. But instead I held it in, as the fog closed in again and he drifted further from the shore we once shared.

These moments—both joyful and shattering—are all part of the same journey. I used to think love was the shared laughter of youth, the whispered dreams in the dark. Now, I know it's also the quiet brushing of his hair. The calm in my voice when I repeat the same answer again and again. It is steering this vessel through fog, with no land in sight—but still steering.

Yes, the fog is real. But so are these glimmers. And as I carry them with me, this fog, this sea, this strange new map of love—it's mine to navigate. And somewhere in the quiet, I'm still here.

Still holding the wheel.

Part I
Roots and Rising:
Early Life, Family, Marriage, and Migration

CHAPTER ONE

---✦---

EARLY LIFE

The Landscape of My Early Life

Since I was young, my father has instilled in my siblings and me a love of nature. Our regular pilgrimage would take us to unknown places. Still, more often than not, we would go to a picturesque mountainous area called Tiger Pass in Chittagong, in East Pakistan, now known as Bangladesh. This sanctuary became home, a refuge and a safe haven for my parents after they migrated in 1949 post-independence. In the tranquil hours before twilight, we went to the forest to bathe and heard the enchanting howls of wolves as they sang in unison, like singers in a grand church choir. Like devout worshippers attending their congregational prayers, they never missed a day. It was ethereal, yet strangely satisfying, as we felt deeply connected to nature's post-golden hour hymns and melodies. Each day, I clasped my father's hands ever so tightly, and with every tightening sensation, I was reminded that he's my protector and that there was no fortress of serenity or tranquillity like being cradled in a father's loving embrace, veiled from life's uncertainties.

Childhood in Chittagong bought its own charms, with tempests, storms and gales making a regular, unsolicited appearance. A vivid memory emerges of me making regular trips to the sea only in my bright blue raincoat and matching boots. My younger sister, in her vibrant, rose-coloured, and slightly red-hued boots. She was always the bolder and more vibrant sister, from her bohemian and eccentric attire right down to the intricacies of her personality. One afternoon, while my mum was having her afternoon siesta, my dad buttoned us in our waterproof gear and guided us to the terrace to enjoy the rain while we took shelter. It was the most memorable afternoon we had together as we revelled in the perfectly orchestrated pitter-patter of raindrops under our mantle of safety and canopy refuge. Following every outing, my father's fondness for nature grew exponentially. Every outing was a sensory exhibition and an adventure that unravelled before our eager eyes. It became instilled in us—a firm understanding and appreciation that we are stewards on this earth. It was created with one mission: to look after it and everything in it. We were taught to protect every living animal, from the largest to the most diminutive creatures, including the ant.

In 1959, my parents relocated to Karachi, in West Pakistan. The purpose was to settle some private business matters with my uncles and be near my paternal grandparents. The relocation blossomed into reconnecting with the ancestral dots of a larger, interconnected extended family, including uncles, aunts, and more than a dozen cousins. Growing up with these youngsters was a fulfilling and joyful experience, marked by a sense of togetherness, albeit accompanied by a healthy dose of bickering that often left us resentful and locked away in our rooms for hours. My dad, who was the patriarch, commanded an air of subtle respect while still being the friendliest character of the bunch and a great storyteller. The night felt young, and my cousins always stayed past midnight, as the gossip and banter never ceased.

When I was a young adolescent, I frequently visited Gandhi Gardens, a local zoo in the city of Karachi, now recognised as Karachi Zoo, situated in the Garden East of Sindh, Pakistan. This zoo haven was first established in 1899 and became a fortnightly pilgrimage for me and my family. It was our idea to visit the best toy store and pick out the best and latest toys. As we drove between the long, stoic, slender trees, I eagerly waited for the appearance of the petite lion cubs, giraffes and, most endearingly, the boisterous, energetic, yet playful chimpanzees. These monkeys loved to reside in treetops and made unexpected yet speedy charges towards us with the fence in between. We loved to tease them with our imaginary gestures as we observed their eager, darting glances. We loved having them as near as possible to the caged fence and would do everything in our power to get as close to them as possible.

In the course of our adventure, we found ourselves captivated by the enchanting journey of an ostrich egg from the moment it was laid to its eventual hatching. This transformative experience turned our mundane routines into a sacred ritual, unfolding narratives of genesis and new beginnings. Week after week, unknown to whom the ostrich egg belonged, we were emotionally attached and felt the need to check in for any updates. The size of the ostrich egg, which amounted to twenty times the size of a chicken's egg, never ceased to amaze me. I had never seen something so big. Each week, post supper and before bedtime, my mind would wander, entranced by the possibility that a baby ostrich was about to hatch and I could possibly negotiate an adoption plan with its owner.

Each of my birthdays was celebrated at Hawkes Bay and Sandspit, the nearest seaside locations to us and our family. It became a family tradition to have a picnic prepared beside the cerulean hues of the sea that stretched endlessly before us, the high tides dancing harmoniously with the coastal breeze.

The sea, with open arms, welcomed all the spectators who stood by the shore. The sound of every tide, the cawing of birds working like a balm, healing and calming the mind, body and soul. Walking barefoot in the golden soil was a grounding, enchanting, and meditative experience; it was warm, gritty, and luring as I felt every tingle beneath my toes. In the blissful tales of these former memories, building sandcastles became a sound ritual. With unbridled joy, my siblings and I would clasp hands and charge towards the waves as they rose, rolled, danced and crashed against the pebbles. The unpredictability of the white saliva attempting to engulf us as we screamed collectively and jolted back to our picnic spread, our laughter blending with the echo of the cerulean waves. With each choppy splash, it was ready to expeditiously engulf our tiny bodies entirely. In our coastal explorations, we consider ourselves extremely fortunate to stumble upon coastal treasures, ideally unbroken and whole.

Taking turns, we would listen to the sounds of the shells, which we believed were Mother Nature's symphony, sharing her trove of wonders and secrets. These oceanic gems came in different shapes, colours, and sizes, but my favourite was the caramel-twirled ones. Our selection process was thorough, as we sought the best of nature's echo of the sea. We chose the ones in pristine condition and took them home with us. I dusted each piece meticulously, turning them into bohemian centrepieces in my bedroom, my sanctuary and cocoon of dreams, alongside the makeshift driftwood that lay seamlessly.

In the realm of education and career, I thrived, meeting the expectations set by my family growing up. Education was not just an arbitrary pursuit but a cherished privilege—one that I certainly did not take for granted. Amid the numerous professions to choose from, I opted to become a teacher, setting the stage for a lifetime commitment to fostering a love of knowledge in young minds.

The genesis of my teaching odyssey started on a balmy winter evening, where luck had me meet Haroon, who had just moved into our neighbourhood, only two blocks away. Families living in this part of Karachi had young children in their early years, with mothers who had not spoken a single word of English. Yet, from this vibrant tapestry emerged Haroon. At the age of four, he joined a nearby Montessori school, where he was eager to master the English language. However, the school fell short of his aspirations, and he needed further assistance. Fuelled by a sense of duty, I stepped in to become his tutor, dedicating a weekly rendezvous in my home to nurture his linguistic skills via regular conversations and writing exercises. With each class, I could see the progress Haroon was making and the glimmer of confidence and hope that sparkled in his eyes. It was one of life's most gratifying and rewarding moments, knowing I could make a difference. In this altruistic endeavour, I found my passion in helping young people unlock their passion for learning. This realisation became a catalyst for my soon-to-be half-century-long career in teaching. As the years unfolded, I built not only classrooms of knowledge but sanctuaries of growth where community, friendship and familial bonds flourished.

Young minds were kindling their innate curiosity and thirst for knowledge.

Matriarchy

My mum, who was a self-sacrificing martyr and warrior, taught me the importance of self-reliance, which encompassed everything from sewing and knitting to cooking and gardening. These skills served me well, even after retirement. They were not just skills but pockets of peace and moments to savour even after retirement. In our world, retirement was a non-existent phenomenon, as there was always something to do. Something to keep our minds and hands busy from dawn till dusk.

My mother was an undeniably strong matriarchal figure who embodied the strength and resilience of her mother, grandmother and all the women who came before her. She taught me the importance of self-reliance and being competent in the domestic sphere. Competency in this area translated into a functional home built on robust pillars that support an entire family, a microcosm of society. From an early age, I learned to sew, knit, cook, garden and read, each skill infused with tireless days of learning and observing the very best. She would sit beside me and guide me with such patience and grace, sharing stories of our family's history with each passing moment. Cooking became a ritual, the act of passing down a recipe that would continue to live in our homes. It was the transforming of simple ingredients into hearty, wholesome meals made with love, each recipe a testament to our heritage and labour of love. My cooking skills were also sharpened during a challenging time in our lives. When my mother became ill, I, as the eldest daughter, found myself stepping into a more responsible role at a young age—just fifteen years old. With my mother's guidance,

I began preparing meals for the family, learning the rhythm of the kitchen while shouldering the responsibility of feeding us all. It was a time that pushed me to grow up quickly, but it also deepened my bond with my mother as we worked together, even as her strength waned.

These crafts were more than hobbies; they were a lifeline, connecting me to generations of South Asian women who had come before us. They were traditions, like treasured heirlooms passed from one generation to the next. My mother had spoken fondly of her mother, who hand-stitched every piece of cloth that her children dressed in and the ornaments around the house. She washed every piece of clothing by hand and prepared every spice mix, as well as an array of pickled and fermented foods and herbal teas for our sick days. These hands are not just for nurturing others but for creating and sustaining life. Even after retirement, women never truly retired; they continued to care for their plants, harvesting ingredients one by one. They were either hosting or volunteering in the community or taking on new projects that stimulated their creativity, selflessness and sense of purpose. The minds and hands were never idly still but remained active until the end. Over time, I came to understand that every recipe, meal, harvest, and stitch sewn was not mere trivial domesticity but an expression of identity, resilience, and love.

At the tender age of twenty- three, I stood at the threshold of adulthood, eagerly anticipating the lifelong companionship that marriage promised. For a woman in the '70s, especially one hailing from a South Asian background, society dictated that after completing your education, marriage was the next logical step.

CHAPTER TWO

---❖---

MARRIAGE

Proposals

Most proposals came through my mother's friends and relatives, who had a large social circle. Usually, family weddings were perfect settings for matchmaking, where mothers, aunties and friends would introduce their daughters and make discreet enquiries. As was customary in our community, mothers of eligible young men would discreetly reach out, often asking, "Can you recommend a suitable girl for my son?" The requests were always the same: they wanted someone beautiful, tall, well-educated, and, of course, a good cook. In those moments, I couldn't help but feel invisible. I never thought I stood a chance, especially when compared to my sister and cousins, who were fair-skinned and effortlessly met the traditional ideals of beauty. Their looks seemed to place them in the running, while I, with my darker complexion, often felt like I was on the sidelines, unsure if I could ever measure up to the standards they set.

I was never short of proposals while I was in Karachi; I was customarily introduced to countless young bachelors who had shown interest in me. Some of them had come to see me with their mothers, who were like their right-hand man in this matchmaking process. The conversations were often formulaic and awkward, as the mother went through a never-ending, painstakingly long checklist of questions around education, hobbies, interests, and, of course, culinary skills. I was directly asked if I knew how to make a biryani. Was I willing to give up my career for my husband?

I learned that I was selected at my brother's wedding six months before mine.

Photographs and Fate

Maa, Qayum's mum, had requested a photo of me for Qayum, which she said she would post for him to see. Of course, he would want a picture of me—after all, he had a right to see who he might be considering for marriage. The pressure was building. I couldn't help but feel that this single photo could determine my future. I scrambled through old albums, hoping to find something that might make a good impression. Finally, I came across a picture from my brother's wedding. I had dressed up for the occasion—smart, polished, and made-up—but my expression was anything but warm. I looked serious, almost stern, and I couldn't shake the fear that this photo might send the wrong message, that it might scare Qayum off before he even had a chance to know me.

I was wearing a simple, elegant shalwar kameez—tasteful and understated, just right for the event, but nothing too flashy. As a family, we decided to send it anyway, hoping for the best. Still, I couldn't shake the feeling that it would be rejected. I had turned down a few proposals myself, after all, so I was prepared for disappointment. But a small part of me still clung to the faint hope that maybe—just maybe—this time would be different.

The sons would do a complete handover to their mums as they had entrusted them to do the thorough checks. At times, I felt like an item at an auction, being appraised to the highest bidder, with every question chipping away at my sense of worth. Yet, I had little to worry about; on paper, I was a graduate of St Joseph's College in Karachi, which was equivalent to any other privileged educational institution at the time. Being an educated woman at the time set a fine precedent and was certainly deemed favourable. Although I didn't possess the conventional beauty of fair skin and coloured eyes, I had all the qualities to be a good wife. I had the fundamental skills of a fine homemaker and nurturer, and I understood the sanctity of marriage and the duties I needed to uphold to make the union flourish.

Maa, was a fair, tall, intelligent lady with a friendly disposition. She walked in with his photo with an oozing sense of pride in her son. With a beaming smile, she assured me that I was a lucky girl to marry her son, as she boasted of the numerous qualities he possessed, from his exceptionally sociable nature to his friendly and generous nature, a man who would light up every room he entered. She described his philanthropic nature as that of a man who would lend a hand when someone was in need and who would be the first to make a sad person smile. As she spoke, I couldn't help but think of the saying that every mother sees the best in her children and naturally downplays all their flaws.

"Of course, he's not perfect," she laughed, "but who is? The main qualities are there, my dear. His heart is so big, he is caring, and that's all that matters." As life throws all its challenges your way, you can rely on him being a shoulder to lean on. I recognised this sentiment in many mothers who had gone through the process of painting their sons as trophy husbands.

Maa's enthusiasm wasn't just about Qayum but the unconditional love of a mother who was protective over her son, wanting to see him in the care of a loving and devoted wife.

The First Spark

I looked at his photo, and at first glance, I couldn't help but be drawn to Qayum. I was captivated by his striking charm and aura. Broadly built, at 5'8", he had a well-proportioned physique that was a testament to his dedication to leading a more active lifestyle. He looked sophisticated in his suit, reflecting his attention to detail and great sense of style. His fair skin and deep hazel eyes sparkled with warmth; it felt inviting and genuine, as if they had a story to share.

But beyond his striking physique, there was a sense of calm that came over me when I looked at this photo. He was bathed in thriving foliage amid a backdrop of lush greenery and daffodil galore. The bold and unmistakable pine trees towered as guardians, watching over Qayum. It was clear he was a calm and passionate soul who had a deep appreciation for nature, a true child of the earth. This was a massive bonus to me on paper, and it made it easy for me to envisage how he was my kindred spirit.

At that moment, I felt an otherworldly connection beyond the physical realm. My soul was drawn to his, a spiritual connection that transcended mere attraction. I could imagine us as an elderly couple, roaming around in nature, hand in hand, sharing muses and life epiphanies. The thought of this handsome stranger becoming my husband was an exciting prospect—one that stirred a flutter of excitement in my stomach. I suppose this is what they mean by "getting butterflies"?

Turning Over a New Page

It was a crisp winter day on December 2nd, 1972, when I first met Abdul Qayum—a day that marked our lifelong commitment and sacred bond.

Qayum entered my life in the most unexpected manner, his entry point weaving a tale of fate and connection that surpassed the conventional and clichéd story. He was already strangely an acquaintance, a thread that was connected to our lives. My family knew his family through my cousin, who had received a proposal from Abdul Qayum, but for reasons unbeknownst to us, the proposal was declined. Years passed, but the thread was still connected; Qayum's proposal had arrived at my doorstep. In the beginning, all I was excited about was the prospect of travelling to London to pursue a Master's; a dream which materialised twenty-three years later, in 1996. The path may have been protracted, but the delay was of little importance against the backdrop of what I had triumphantly achieved.

My marriage to Abdul Qayum was arranged through a time-honoured tradition and common, customary practice, despite being frequently misunderstood and erroneously labelled as a "forced marriage", with the bride having no say whatsoever. However, this was far from the truth, for my voice was never diminished but rather encouraged at every stage leading up to the marriage and throughout the marriage itself.

A Promise for Life

There are not many people who leave a resounding impression on you, but my husband was the exception. I often wondered how a stranger showed more unwavering commitment and loyalty to me than all of my friends combined. Abdul Qayum came from

London to marry a faceless entity who would soon become the most familiar face and entity in his life. He chose commitment over curiosity, faithfulness over inquiry, and allegiance over wonder. The only approval he needed was from his most trusted advisor, his mother, and for him, this sufficed. While I had only seen his picture, Qayum was not afforded the same privilege lest he refused the proposal.

The consequences were far greater than a mere rejection but rather a dishonour to his mother and the wider community. Adhering to her promise was imperative, as any deviation or altercation would bring shame to both families.

Maa wanted me to be her son's partner for life, a compliment as Qayum was her favourite among her six boys. She had told me with unwavering confidence that I would be the perfect match for him, but I didn't fully understand what that meant. She spoke with such certainty as though there could be no doubt in her mind, and I never gave her a reason to question it.

Growing up as a Pakistani girl in a conservative Muslim household in the late 1960s, my world was carefully defined by the values of our faith and culture. I didn't know any boys. My education was confined to an all-girls school and college, where my interactions with boys were non-existent. Even my male cousins were distant figures in my life; our relationships with them were shaped by tradition and were always formal, respectful, and distant. In such an environment, the concept of choosing a partner was something I had been taught to surrender to my parents.

I had no experience navigating matters of the heart, nor was I allowed to. So, when it came time to make a decision about my future, I did what I had always been taught to do: I placed my complete trust in their hands, knowing that their judgement—

shaped by faith, culture, and family—was my guiding light. It was a different time, a different way of living, but for me, it was all I had ever known.

Several months were spent planning for the big day. My mother, although lacking in formal education, was gifted domestically—a prowess and gift that showed as she took responsibility for my dowry, also known as a trousseau. This typically encompassed twenty-four-carat jewellery pieces, occasionwear such as sarees and fine everyday pieces, as well as basic wardrobe staples. One of the remarkable talents my mum possessed among her numerous gifts was her ability to craft delicate jewellery sets for me. Although she did not attend school after the age of twelve, she was schooled differently, with many teachers coming in to teach her embroidery, knitting and pattern making. As a result, her fine and sophisticated craft meant she was able to create unique pieces for my dowry collection.

The dowry system had deep roots in Indian society, even before the British colonisation; it was a customary practice stemming from ancient Hindu traditions and customs. The idea behind this system was to ensure the bride would be financially stable after getting married. The Hindus did not give their daughters any share of the family property; instead, they were given dowries in the form of household utilities for the newlyweds' new home. The intention was very clear, but in recent times, it has created problems in society. Over time, the groom's family would ask for everything from a home to a car, subsequently leaving poor parents unable to marry their daughters without breaking the bank. It became common practice for families to go into debt, take loans or even sell their everyday items. What was once a sacred partnership built on mutual respect, harmony, and devotion morphed into a transactional arrangement. My mum, like many other mothers, followed this established practice, and sadly, it remains widely practised to this day.

Karachi Bazaars

We went to the bazaars almost every day, but no one navigated them quite like my mum. She moved through the labyrinth of crowded streets with the ease of someone who had lived them for a lifetime. She knew every shopkeeper by name, every twist and turn of the narrow, winding alleys, and every single product that filled the bustling stalls. The bazaars were a sensory overload: a riot of vibrant colours, from the rich reds and golds of fabric to the bright oranges and greens of fresh produce. Everywhere you looked, there was something to catch your eye, something that seemed to pulse with life.

The air was thick with the heady aromas of street food, the spicy heat of sizzling samosas, the crisp crunch of golden pakoras, and the intoxicating blend of cumin, coriander, and garam masala. It was impossible to walk through without your mouth watering, your senses completely overwhelmed by the warmth and richness of the smells. The cacophony of voices—the calls of shopkeepers, the murmur of bargaining, the laughter of children running through the crowds—blended together in a symphony of life.

Karachi's bazaars were a world unto themselves, where the old and new collided. You could find intricately woven, hand-embroidered shawls alongside the latest international fashion brands. The sheer variety was dizzying, and yet it felt like everything belonged in this vibrant melting pot of tradition and modernity. My mum, with her sharp eye for detail, seemed to thrive here. She would spend hours haggling, negotiating, and carefully selecting each item for the wedding, her sense of purpose guiding her through the madness. She knew where to find the best deals, which vendor offered the freshest ingredients, and which stall held the perfect items for the wedding preparations.

Her attention to detail was meticulous, and though the chaos of the bazaar could be overwhelming to anyone else, it was clear to us that she was in complete control. Her organisation and her ability to juggle dozens of tasks at once were unparalleled. We knew, without a shadow of a doubt, that she had everything under control for the wedding. No detail would be overlooked. No request would go unmet. In the midst of the bustling marketplace, amid the sensory overload of sound, sight, and smell, my mum was a force of nature—a woman who knew exactly what she wanted and how to get it.

Qayum arrived a couple of days before the big day. I wanted to be at the airport to see him from a distance, so I made plans with my uncle Taher, who had encouraged me to travel with him on his motorbike. The secret mission came to a halt instantly, however, as a family member leaked the information, I was reprimanded for my apparent unacceptable behaviour. It was at that moment that I came to accept that I wasn't going to see my husband until the wedding day.

A Leap of Love

The long-awaited day had finally arrived for my Nikkah, also referred to as the Islamic marriage, the day the union between two strangers was formalised in front of witnesses, who in our case were Qayum's brothers and my dad's brothers. They were required to be there by Islamic law to formalise the marriage, attesting to the bride and groom showing unequivocal Qubool, as they both willingly embraced their union before God. Following the Nikkah, the festivities continued with the Pakistani Shaadi or wedding reception, which was a larger celebration. By large, this was approximately five hundred guests, including neighbours, friends and so-called relatives who had been absent from our lives for the last decade or so. Having all our family and friends come under one roof made the day profoundly more memorable.

On my wedding day, I adorned myself with a white Banarasi saree, a garment that women across the Indian subcontinent typically took pride in wearing. The fabric, made from the finest silk, gracefully adorning my figure, was five to seven yards long, heavily embroidered in the most intricate and luxurious gold and silver. Completing the look was the khombi, which was a head cover, dupatta or veil covering crafted by the finest hands using the tie and dye technique to create a tapestry of hues draped over my head and shoulders. Traditionally, they were red and black in colour with delicate white dotted patterns like dainty flecks or whisper-soft markings.

I also wore a shiny patterned gold tikka on my forehead, a staple piece many South Asian women wore between the middle part of their hair, with a pendant that adorned my forehead. While traditionally worn by brides for its sheer symbol of glitz and glamour, many women considered it a cherished piece for all ages.

As I looked at my reflection, my face was laden with makeup like a porcelain doll. I was never accustomed to a full face, but if there was any day to look fully glammed, this was the day. My hands and feet were blank canvases festooned with a myriad of swirls and twirls that told old tales of tradition and celebration.

The Big Reveal

Qayum walked onto the stage with his family. My heart was thumping, my pulse was high, my throat felt dry, and I didn't know what to expect next. I was feeling overwhelmed with thoughts: what if I didn't like him? I was nervous, but I tried to keep myself calm and collected and tried to convince myself that my parents wouldn't give me away to a completely foolish man and my dad's words ringing in my ear, "You will only know him when you live with him." How true is that!

It felt bizarre as Qayum sat next to me on the stage. It was a stranger sitting ever so close to me, shoulder to shoulder, with no eye contact as I was cloyingly seated with my veil over my face. I had never sat next to a stranger of the opposite sex in my life, never mind a man who I was about to call my husband. My cousins brought a large mirror on stage, another old tradition we had, whereby the bride and groom would exchange and reveal their first glances through an external metallic portal. At that moment, the tension in my chest eased, and a sense of calm replaced my worries as I saw Qayum's face, smiling radiantly; his eyes, a window to his compassionate and kind soul, were revealed. My face lit up like a constellation of stars. I knew I was going to be in safe hands. The soft murmurs turned to celebratory clamour and a festive uproar from the guests, sharing this beautiful and intimate moment from the bride and groom.

In anticipation of the next event, I assumed Qayum had no idea what to expect as my cousins indulged in the *Joota Chupai* tradition, which literally means "hiding the shoes". His *mojari*, or handcrafted white leather shoes, were stolen by my cousins as they exchanged them in a jovial ritual, jestingly expecting payment to have his shoes returned. With the dozen or so girls swarming around Qayum and with his shoe taken away, he was demanded a ransom to have his footwear back and to walk me to the car. Fully aware of the customary practices, his younger brother and sister had come prepared. Initially, Qayum gave a modest sum of one hundred rupees. The guests were amused and considered him tightfisted and Scrooge-like, considering he had come from England. However, at every chant, he increased the amount until he reached a thousand rupees, which my female cousins all agreed to share amongst themselves.

In the following weeks, the *Walima*, an Arabic term meaning "feast", was hosted by the groom and his family. This was a much-awaited and special occasion that preceded our trip to Karachi, where we stayed for three weeks. Our families and friends hosted parties for us to celebrate our newlywed stage. During this time, we also got to know each other and our families more closely.

Hitting a New Road

The time had come to say my farewells—to my family, my cousins, my friends, and the neighbours who had been like extended family. I was about to leave for a land I had never seen, a place that felt both distant and foreign, an unfamiliar road. It was then, in that quiet moment of departure, that the full weight of what I was doing hit me. I was leaving behind everything I had ever known—my entire world, my clan. What had I done?

I could hardly bear to look at my father, his silence speaking volumes, a quiet resignation in his eyes. And my mother—how could I leave her like this, with tears silently trailing down her cheeks? The love, the loss, the uncertainty—it was all too much. I felt as if I was tearing myself away from the very roots that had shaped me, and yet, I had no choice but to go. I had to leave it all behind. And in that moment, the reality of it all became painfully clear: I was stepping into the unknown, not just physically, but emotionally as well.

My father kissed me on my forehead and blessed me with a great future; my mum was crying hysterically and, in a choking voice, whispered, "Fi AmaanAllah," meaning "May Allah protect."

A bittersweet feeling lingered, too, however, as these were our people, our tribe we were leaving behind as we ventured into the unknown. Holding hands with my husband, we embarked on our fresh adventure on January 1st 1973.

CHAPTER THREE

---◆---

NEWLYWEDS IN A NEW COUNTRY

In The Clouds

Seated beside Qayum on the flight, I watched the golden hour closely over Karachi airport, a vast canvas setting low below the horizon before metamorphosing into a bleak, ghastly cotton mist, the thick, ebony clouds enveloping the sky. It was the first time I experienced the moody atmosphere, the mystical obscurity of thick, dense, heavy fog that felt cold and dreary. I knew nothing about England beyond its notoriously bad weather and the British people's supposedly dry sense of humour, their stiff upper lip, and their love for tea.

Qayum sensed my feelings and thoughts, held my hand, and then gently whispered, "You will be fine, my dear. Of course, you will miss every single one of them, but I will be here for you always. I will be your family and home." My eyes welled up, and I looked into his eyes, which comforted me with a sense of assurance.

Due to dense fog and heavy snow at Heathrow Airport, our

flight was delayed in Frankfurt, resulting in an overnight stay at the Hilton. I was taken aback by the world we had stepped into. It was modernity on steroids, a contemporary marvel at its finest. A world filled with the intricate dance of sliding doors, the humming of conveyor belts, and escalators ascending and descending in a timely purpose, transporting people to different towering buildings. As I stepped outside, the first thing that struck me was the unusual stillness—every car dutifully came to a stop at the red signals, and the streets were eerily quiet without the constant blare of car horns. I was captivated by the sight of a bustling crowd, faces rushing past me as they all hurried toward the trains, their attention absorbed in newspapers and books. It was a scene I had never experienced before.

All the houses looked the same, neatly and tidily in rows with red tile roofs. The roads were clean and wide, with numerous road signs, creating a completely different world from where I had come from. In the '70s, there was none of the ethereal glow of digital screens that surrounds us today. People were completely engrossed in the tangible world around them, a far cry from the distractions of modern technology.

In this uncharted territory, I felt like a child again, in an unknown city, except with a vigilant and protective guardian who knew the ins and outs of everything. It was in these moments that I felt the unwavering care and support of not only a husband but a life partner who would be there through the ebbs and flows of life, in times of crisis and calm, as well as adversity and prosperity.

Adrift in a Foggy Sea

In the ballad of life, we often echo tales of grief, heartbreak, and loss, yet homesickness remains an unsung note. Little is said of the yearning for home, the feeling of fracture, leaving you in a chronic state of exile from yourself and the world around you.

From the moment I set foot in England, I felt homesick. The excitement of newlywed life seemed to be on hold as I thought less about the budding romance of my honeymoon and the intricate process of assimilating into a whole new culture, identity, and environment. I needed to accustom myself to new habits that were culturally wired, like carrying an umbrella or waterproof jacket at all times, accepting invitations to afternoon tea featuring an abundance of scones, cream cakes and egg and mayo sandwiches, and understanding that the lack of pleasantries or small talk before giving directions did not equate to rude or uncouth behaviour.

Our first temporary crib was Qayum's brother's residence in Wandsworth, which felt nothing like home except for my mother's spice blend, which lingered with the fragrant notes of cardamom, the earthy base of coriander seeds, and the warmth of the garam masala that wafted through the kitchen. More than ever, the craving for a home intensified. I longed for my own space and begged Qayum to move into our own home, even if it was still unfurnished. And without delay, Qayum and I moved to Bradford, also known as the Curry Capital of the UK, just above Habib Bank Ltd, where he worked as a manager.

Every morning, as I peeked outside the window, I was overtaken by a dull canvas of gloom, a blanket of monotony as the skies were overcast, drizzly and dreary. This was a sharp contrast to the bright, warm golden hues that enveloped the vibrant city of Karachi, which I had left behind. Soon, I would become a stranger in my own home as I began leading a new life in the UK.

In the vast, spacious single room, furniture was sparse while our life's possessions and belongings were all tucked away in old-fashioned trunks that seemed weathered not by storms but by the contagion of displacement and uprooting.

New Beginnings

A couple of weeks later, we moved to our permanent home at the time, in Chippendale, Allerton. As soon as we stepped through the door, Qayum wasted no time. He immediately performed the adhaan, followed by two rakahs, which is a short prayer. It is a tradition among Muslims to perform this ritual as a way of cleaning their home from any evil. It is also common to recite or play Surah Al-Baqarah for spiritual protection from any harm.

Number 56 Chippendale Rise was a true reflection of Qayum's fine taste. It was a charming semi-detached property nestled in the heart of Allerton, immersed in acres of lush foliage and botanical richness. The area encompassed the suburbs of Allerton and the village of Thornton, with vast, idyllic fields surrounding Chellow Dene Beck. It was a place where time seemed to slow down, where dark brown stallions and ponies roamed the area, their glossy, sleek coats gleaming as if they had been polished or waxed. It was a truly serene, picturesque and peaceful location with the countryside wrapped around us.

As we slowly settled in, we made frequent visits to the Lake District, specifically to Lake Windermere, England's largest lake, which stretches 10.5 miles. Its captivating vistas invited us to take the longest walks along its waters. Visits to the lakes epitomised the finest British scenery, and we knew Lake District wouldn't let any of our guests down.

A wave of South Asians had arrived in the 1960s as qualified doctors, teachers, engineers, supermarket owners, and butchers.

As immigrants coming into the country, they were coming with skills that were truly invaluable to the economy. Our neighbours were primarily white middle class, with no brown or ethnic person in sight unless I travelled out a bit further into Lumb Lane, which was a miniature Pakistan even in the early seventies.

Fortunately, my English was good, so I was able to converse effectively with anyone I encountered.

The Pakistani community here was a world apart, a tapestry of faces stitched together by a shared mother tongue. Yet, each had their own story of how they uprooted themselves and left their home country. Most of them were surrounded by foreign faces, and an unfamiliar language and homesickness reeked in the air. Their words consisted of a blend of Urdu, Punjabi, and Pashto—languages wrapped in the warmth of sunrise. The UK, in its post-war hunger for diligent workers who could rebuild the country, called out for cheap labour to fuel its industry with the promise of a brighter future. They arrived with hopes that flickered like fragile lanterns in the dark for themselves and their children—a hope for a new beginning of prosperity and abundance. The struggle was not simply about survival but hope to belong to a new land, where cold stares and a stiff upper lip were commonplace—a place they could finally call home.

A Rare Bond

Over the course of our marriage, we grew accustomed to each other. Qayum had the habit of greeting me with salaams every morning as soon as I woke up, which I initially found challenging. I was used to hitting the snooze button several times before fully waking up, so his early greetings caught me off guard. At first, I hated it, and it took me a couple of months before I could finally respond to him. He was an early riser, and I hated my sleep being disturbed. Qayum never needed an alarm to wake him up.

But other gestures of his brought me joy. His charming habit of coming home at lunchtime just to be with me or taking me on long walks to Shipley Glen made me feel loved and appreciated. I also cherished it when he encouraged me to take the bus to Bradford town centre to spend the afternoon, then meet him at the end of the day at his workplace. Those moments meant more to me than I could put into words. We navigated through many of these moments with patience and conversing openly and gently, but a recurrent issue we faced was Qayum's reckless driving. I would worry at times about his extreme road rage, accompanied by his stream of reproaches and expletives, as he tailgated and honked incessantly at some poor, absent-minded teenager crossing the street. Often, I would tap on his thigh and ask him to calm down. His reply was always the same: "Can't you see what he did just now!" Then he would mutter a phrase in Urdu: "Ullu Ka Patha." It's a derogatory expression to describe someone foolish or lacking intelligence, much like how an owl is stereotypically associated with being slow or dim-witted. I couldn't help but wonder why I wasn't warned about this trait before getting married. But in my defence, who would ask a suitor: "Do you experience road rage?" Seriously? Who would answer candidly and honestly with, "No, not at all, I am as calm as a monk behind the wheel!" Technically, I had seen Qayum drive after he married me, but that was in Karachi, where everyone seemed to be going as though they were in a circus. The chaos was palpable.

The truth is, no one advertises their flaws or demons. For this reason, it was simply about accepting that everything comes with risks, given that life is a bundle of imperfections, just like marriage, which is essentially two imperfect people living in an imperfect world, trying to navigate life with love, mercy and compassion imperfectly. And this is where *tawakkul* comes in—trusting that Allah, in His infinite wisdom, would perfectly place you with your imperfect person.

Left Behind

When Qayum left for work and I was alone in the house, the hours stretched before me endlessly, like an endless horizon. I felt a state of profound boredom and a deep hollowness. The emptiness was suffocating and all-consuming. It was as though I was a leaf that was blown away from its tree, lost in an unfamiliar space, constantly longing for home. Qayum was often occupied with work, so I turned to reading the Holy Qur'an and Hadith—not only to spend my time meaningfully, but to seek understanding and spiritual grounding.

Qayum was an empath and did his best to console me. However, I couldn't shake off the feeling that he didn't truly understand how much I was emotionally struggling. I could sense the unspoken resignation and silent defeat in his eyes, the weight of not knowing how to fix this feeling of despair. In those moments, he would express with much enthusiasm, albeit partly in jest, that he would ship my family over from abroad to keep me company. The words were spoken with such tenderness that I couldn't help but appreciate the sentiment behind it, but I also knew it was nothing more than a promise beyond reach.

At times, when I felt pity and sorrow, I remembered the words of Qayum when he was asked by my parents if there was anything he needed. He said, with poetic grace and sound conviction: "You have given me Atiya (a gift, a present), and I shall treasure her forever. There is nothing more I could ask for." I couldn't help but savour the authenticity of his beautiful words, coupled with his undisputed and irrevocable sincerity. Among all the romantic tales, this was the pinnacle moment for me. Tender words, coupled with stalwart commitment and loyalty. Not the half-hearted, cringeworthy tales you hear about, but the rawest of emotions that consisted of committing yourself every day to a spouse, despite their imperfections, flaws and quirks.

Qayum had fine taste in many things, not excluding his fashion, people and hobbies. He was also a polyglot who spoke eight languages—Urdu, Punjabi, Kutchi, Gujarati, Hindi, Bengali, Pashto and English with sophisticated flair. It was truly impressive when, just a week after we had started spending time together, Qayum spoke to my mother in Kutchi. While he primarily communicated in Urdu and English, hearing him switch so effortlessly between languages left a strong impression on me. His job at the bank allowed him to interact with customers from various cities across Pakistan, and he often mentioned how these interactions helped him refine his linguistic abilities. He had mastered the art of seamlessly transitioning from one language to another, a skill for which he took great pride. It was a skill none of our children inherited; the most they had learned at school was French, which, though useful, could not compare to Qayum's remarkable fluency in multiple languages.

Qayum was ever so thoughtful; he treated me to my favourite desserts, fresh cream cakes. He would sweep me away on languid strolls, drives through the countryside, and, for his lunch breaks, come home from his bank in Cheapside, the centre of Bradford Town Centre, just to bask in our shared company. I treasured this thoughtful gesture and made fresh roti to serve with the chicken masala curry I would whip up in under twenty minutes.

Those little pockets of connection each day were so special and nourishing to the soul, deepening my love for Qayum, especially when he would offer comforting words and gestures to ease my loneliness—bringing me magazines and newspapers so I could spend my afternoons immersed in them.

A couple of times, he would say, "I am here just to break the long day for you, to keep you busy preparing lunch for your husband." I felt his genuine care and looked forward to our lunchtimes together. It was such a great blessing, and of course, my attention was diverted.

As soon as Qayum entered the house, he would cast aside the weight of the world and offer his *salam*. A comforting melody that would echo through the halls. It was a ritual as familiar as the rising sun and one that would never go amiss. Life's beauty lies in its simplicity. Qayum's greeting was often enough to put me in a better mood for the rest of the evening. Reminding myself of the blessing of having a devoted, loving and compassionate man who was my husband. His warmth radiated at all times; his kindness served as a balm to my homesickness, wrapping me in a warm comfort. These moments were sacrosanct, like the familiarity that oozed from my mother's masala chai when I was recovering from an ailment or the symphony of rhythmic raindrops that patterned against the roof deck of my mother's veranda.

With a tender smile that would light up any room he entered, he'd gently enquire about my health and whether I had been lonely in his absence. His genuine concern was so palpable I could hear it in every vowel and syllable. I would, of course, take the opportunity to unleash a storm of words his way, complaining about the dull weather, the lack of spontaneity with social interactions and some customs that felt contrived and mundane at times.

CHAPTER FOUR

———�֍———

FAMILY LIFE BEGINS

The Good News

Discovering that I was having a child marked a special moment, one that is expected in every ethnic home. The countdown begins on the wedding day, preceding the inundation of uncouth and unsolicited enquiries. In cases where couples decide to delay or put this stage off, concerns start to surface from family and extended family about fertility issues or some other impending issues.

For us, we were ever so happy with the news, more so Qayum, for he had always been so family-oriented and paternal. It wasn't customary practice for the wife to announce her pregnancy, and so the much-awaited news came from Qayum.

The joy quickly morphed into morning sickness, or rather all-day sickness, which felt like a new, permanent version of myself: chronically nauseous, woozy and lethargic. The relentless nausea left me feeling vulnerable and in a state of anxiety; my body was teetering between fight or flight mode, unaware of when the moment of doom would come about, and I would vomit everything I had just eaten. All I was left with was digested food, bile and a sour aftertaste in my mouth. The idea of smells became repulsive, causing my stomach to convulse.

I had already noticed the changes in Qayum as he transitioned into fatherhood. I saw an ever more considerate and selfless side. He quit smoking, not just for me, but for the growing child inside me. He also became a lot more mindful on the road, conscious of my susceptibility to car sickness.

More importantly, Qayum curated a literary treasure for me on childbirth and parenting. His thoughtful selection was aimed at equipping me with the necessary knowledge and finer intricacies of parenting. Still, the book I remember to this day was Dr Spock's *Pregnancy Guide*, which served as a seminal text in the literary canon of this discipline.

The book emerged as an unexpected yet cherished companion in the nine months of carrying my beautiful child, a precious promise of a new life. Its pages were inked with wisdom and sacred lessons about my body and the changes it was about to endure. It took me through a roadmap of my body's transformation. Yet, amid these pages of wisdom and poignant lessons, I could not help but miss the maternal figures who stood with unwavering strength like pillars in our lives, the sacrificial martyrs, unsung heroes and stoic soldiers who carried the weight of mountains without ever complaining. These were the women whose footsteps I longed to follow during my vulnerability and despair.

With a renewed sense of purpose, I knew I wanted to delve into this new phase of life wholeheartedly. I wanted to do God's work with due diligence. From the first tender kick, I fell in love with my child. It was a feeling of home in my chronic state of homesickness and the blossoming spring following the desolate symphony of a harsh winter. I was frequently warned that the sense of unconditional love would only ever be truly experienced by a mother for her child—an undeniable connection and an enduring bond that a husband would adore yet crave for himself. To keep myself busy, I began knitting blankets, mittens, sweaters and sleep sacks. I wanted every item to carry sentimental value, serving as heirlooms for her siblings and my grandkids. It was the first labour of love and a way of infusing warmth and love into the fabric of my child's early life.

In this life-altering chapter, an unexpected event unfolded: the *Godh Bharai*, which in Indian tradition literally translates to "fill the lap" with abundance. This ceremony is held in the seventh month of pregnancy. The mother-to-be is showered with gifts, including exquisite saree pieces, jewellery and fruits for nourishment. Qayum and I were reluctant to carry it out, given that it did not align with our religious beliefs.

June ushered in my first birthday with Qayum, and yet nothing could have prepared me for the oppressive shadow that set over me that summer. The nostalgic echoes of belly laughs at the seaside were long gone. Instead, I was sitting almost double, curled against my bed, ruminating depressive and dark thoughts. There were no well wishes or presents, only silent tears. Qayum had forgotten my birthday, and that was a feeling I couldn't shake off. How could he forget? When I finally put my pride aside and mentioned it in passing, he nonchalantly told me the onus was on me to remind him. In his defence, he never remembered any birthdays, not even his own or those of his parents or children. So I consoled myself with the fact that my husband is just like many other men, clueless in this department.

The summer felt longer than ever, and the days felt dreary. I was only a few weeks away from the delivery date, on September 21st. I gave Qayum a shopping list in the morning before he left for work, hoping to stock up the freezer with the necessary staples. That afternoon, my water broke. There were no contractions or immense pain—it felt seamless. However, I knew this was temporary until the contractions worsened like a storm.

Qayum, with his unruffled demeanour and stoic composure, was evidently not the one who was carrying a child. We had dinner together, and it was then I started to show symptoms of early labour. I felt the contractions, which I always knew were like periods on steroids. Fortunately, the Bradford Royal Infirmary was only a five-minute drive away from our home. I took my maternity bag, which I had packed a few weeks ago, and headed straight to the hospital with Qayum, who was consoling me to stay calm. Actually, Qayum really didn't have a clue what to expect.

A Precious Gift

On September 1st, we were blessed with a beautiful baby girl, Amber. She was a petite and exquisite baby, weighing six pounds and two ounces. She embodied the beauty of both her paternal and maternal grandmothers, with fair skin, light hair, and hazel eyes. However, she subtly resembled her father the most, with her "Bambi eyes" that sparkled every time she smiled and her soft, light, auburn, curly hair. She took nothing from me.

Qayum welcomed us in the hospital with a sea of red roses, which filled the hospital room. Tears streamed down my cheeks, releasing a flood of serotonin that made me feel an immense feeling of bliss, reverberating through my bones as I cradled my beautiful angel in my arms. The labour felt like an eternity, with every minute stretched into an hour. Following my mother's advice, I recited Surah Al-Fatiha, the opening chapter of the Qur'an, to fortify my strength during one of life's most transformative life events. It was all worth it though. As I lay there with Amber nestled in my arms, our chests pressed together, I felt her warm breath against mine, each little heartbeat a symphony to my ears. Her delicate hands and miniature feet cradled against mine, creating a bond too deep for words.

Qayum devoted himself to me fully during my pregnancy and early stages of motherhood. I was treated to gold milk and platters of fruit—especially an assortment of my favourites: blackcurrant, passion fruit—and leisurely strolls around Yorkshire's picturesque scenery, including Ilkley Moor, Shipley Glen, the Peak District, and the Brontë country. Amber came into our lives and completely changed the dynamics, as any child does. She was a colicky baby, and it was heartbreaking seeing her in pain and constantly screaming. Exhaustion crept in, and for the next few months, our focus shifted entirely to keeping our baby well and comfortable.

Amber demanded a lot of attention, compromising daily feeds, nappy changes, teething and visits to the local clinic. Back then, there was no paternity leave, but thankfully, Qayum managed to take six weeks off to take care of me and Amber. Qayum was resourceful and devoted and took it in his stride to tend to our needs. In my case, it was the postpartum struggles of physical exhaustion, cravings and the joys of hormones taking over, with occasional mood swings. But Qayum let me rest and recover while he put Amber in her pram and took her out for fresh air. Qayum went against the grain, as men in Karachi typically adhered to gendered stereotypes and avoided looking after the children. Thankfully, Qayum wasn't typical and unique in that sense and advocated for women's rights, including their right to be cared for unconditionally, especially while dealing with postpartum. I would often compliment Qayum, affirming what a wonderful example he was setting for our future children and how his actions aligned with our prophetic teachings rather than ingrained belief systems and cultural practices.

In the backdrop of the 1970s, it was customary for mothers and mothers-in-law to be the proud grandmas they were and show off their love and affection for the grandchild by helping out with the mother's duties. Their focus was letting the mother rehabilitate and recover from labour while attending to their grandchild. It was typical for the mother to be pampered during this time—cooked for and massaged, and in the ninth month, the mother would retreat to her parents' home to deliver the baby and receive all the family's love and care.

However, my experience was a stark contrast to what I had hoped for. Once Qayum returned to work, with its long hours at the bank, I was left alone, caring for Amber. By the evening, I was completely exhausted. In those moments, I truly understood the meaning of the famous adage, "It takes a village to raise a child". This lifestyle, which had felt so normal back home, was something I left behind when I came to the UK.

Eid Away

It was not long till Ramadan came. Qayum observed his fasts with unwavering dedication. Each morning, before the first light of dawn, he would wake up for *suhoor* to make a hearty meal that would keep him going throughout the long day of fasting. He was like clockwork every morning. I would know he was awake because of the soft clink of plates and the sizzle of frying eggs.

I focused on Amber's feeds, changing her nappies and making *iftar*.

The days got increasingly difficult as Qayum and I were both waking up at odd hours to feed and comfort Amber. I felt I was more committed to my faith than Qayum. I had fasted for the first time when I was only twelve years old, and I had been committed to fasting every day since then.

At the end of Ramadan, the celebrations of Eid ul-Fitr marked the culmination of a month of strife and sacrifice. Every Muslim around the world celebrated this day with much vigour and excitement. It was a day of sweets galore, vibrant clothing, families coming together, and children eagerly awaiting their gifts and money. It was a precious wish of mine to see every Muslim celebrate Eid collectively on the same day. But alas, the sighting of the moon was never in sync, and no two observers ever seemed to agree. This led to the tongue-in-cheek term "Moon Wars", which humorously describes the endless disagreements people had around the world over the lunar calendar. On the morning of Eid, we recited prayers on our way to the mosque for the congregational prayer. We repeated "Allahu Akbar", which is a way of glorifying God as part of the *sunnah*, or Prophetic tradition. It was my first Eid away from home, and the weight of homesickness pressed down on me. I had no neighbours, cousins or friends who were popping in unannounced to check up on my well-being or to break bread. There was no *mithai*, no vermicelli in milk loaded with almonds and pistachios. How could it possibly be Eid? To make matters worse, Qayum was working on Eid day so that his other colleagues could take the day off to celebrate Eid with their families. The irony. It was a selfless act indeed, and I knew I needed to be equally considerate and acknowledge his generosity. But at that moment, I couldn't contend with my feelings, knowing I had no one besides Qayum to celebrate Eid with. Alas, he eventually made it home that evening with some *mithai*, which we thoroughly enjoyed. To accompany that, I made *biryani*—a traditional staple dish served at Eid and Asian weddings.

Karachi Bound

My first visit back to Karachi was in December of 1974. I went with my daughter only. Unfortunately, Qayum was unable to join as he had no days remaining on his annual leave. Although I was initially disappointed, I could see the silver lining. I knew I needed some time away to recharge my batteries and embrace the feeling of unconditional love and the familiar comfort of home with no strings attached. Before leaving, I meticulously cooked a few of Qayum's favourite meals and popped them in the freezer for him to access at his convenience. I'd hoped for some acknowledgement or words of affirmation before my departure, but instead, he dismissed me, saying that he'd lived for thirteen years without any supervision or care and that he was going to be fine on his own. His words upset me, as I felt that neither my absence nor my presence meant enough to him.

As I stepped off the plane, my heart raced with gleeful anticipation at the sight of my family. The airport was bustling with people, the metallic clinks and rolling thuds of suitcases being dragged along smooth tile floors. But all I could think about was my father. I longed to see him. From childhood, I had always had a special bond with him—his presence was a comfort to me, a silent reassurance that I had a protective guardian watching over me at all times.

My eyes scanned the crowd. I searched for the man with kind eyes who would be eagerly awaiting to see his beloved daughter.

But he wasn't there. I felt a sinking feeling in my stomach, a knot of unease twisted inside me, and my jaw clenched. Everyone else was there—except him. It felt... empty.

My brother's and sister's faces were warm and kind but reserved, as though something was being held back. I instantly saw the unspoken words in their eyes. "Dad's unwell," they solemnly conveyed. "He's gutted he couldn't make it, but he sends his well wishes." The weight of their words hit me like a punch in the gut. The reunion I had envisaged was slowly slipping away, unravelling, replaced by an unsettling silence, faces clouded with sorrow.

My mind raced, playing out a thousand worst-case scenarios. Every scenario was worse than the other. Then, the words finally came, slow and heavy. "Dad had undergone retinal surgery," Mum said, her voice tight. "But it's gone terribly wrong... He... He's lost his eyesight."

I froze. I couldn't breathe. My dad was... blind?

My heart shattered into a million pieces, a deep ache spreading through my body, my legs shaking and feeling weak. I was lightheaded, disorientated and feeling faint, as though I was trapped in a nightmare that I couldn't escape from. I wanted to scream, but no words came to mind.

No one had warned me about the feeling of visiting your own home after marriage, especially after being a homebody once. The strange feeling of being a stranger in your own space—like a temporary visitor who has to leave and return to her new "home", which she is responsible for. It felt like nothing had changed, yet the dynamics had shifted with all the attention now focused on Amber. My dearest mum knew I was there for a limited time and wanted to cherish every moment together by preparing many of my favourite meals. This was how my mum expressed her love to us.

Relatives came to visit, and the winter night gatherings were lively, bustling and familiar. Conversations flowed freely, and my light-heartedness and freestyle jokes came flooding back. Some commented that I was no longer the Atiya they remembered, which I received in jest. With a smile, I replied that was inevitable, given that marriage is a transformative dynamic—one unlike any other. It gently reshapes you inviting growth, compromise and shared purpose. With all its hardships and struggles, using light-hearted humour as a coping mechanism brought immense comfort. It served as a gentle reminder not to lose yourself, or your authenticity, amidst the traumas and projections of the other person.

Qayum's first letter tugged at my heartstrings. It read: "It's only been a week, and I am feeling lonelier than ever without you and Amber by my side. It is an undeniable truth that your presence infuses our home with comforting familial warmth and echoes of laughter."

His words were extremely romantic and witty, effortlessly drawing me into a cascade of belly laughs and cheerful chortles. It was his intelligence that stood out to me—a remarkable quickness of mind that never failed to charm. I assured Qayum that I would be back very soon, despite my initial desire for an extended sojourn in the comforting embrace of my childhood home. I found myself longing for Qayum—someone I now associated with the feeling of home, my new and enduring sanctuary. Accompanying the letter was a delicate pearl necklace, its iridescent glow perfectly symbolising the celebration of my second wedding anniversary. Qayum never missed an anniversary, treasuring each one with unwavering devotion for the years to come.

New Additions

I was often the target of playful jests about having so many children that I might one day field a cricket team. But every time Qayum joked about it, he was met with a firm shake of my head. He didn't understand the quiet war raging inside me at the mere thought. I knew my body—fragile and already worn from the trials of motherhood—couldn't bear the weight of more than three or four pregnancies.

The idea alone filled me with an overwhelming dread. It wasn't just the physical strain—the tearing, the swelling, the nausea that gnawed at me each morning—but the deeper truth: the unspoken cost of giving life. No amount of support could lighten the crucible of pain, the relentless sacrifice etched into the journey of motherhood. It was a commitment that stretched far beyond the moment of birth, tethering me to that life until my last breath. To be a mother was to endure, to give endlessly until there was nothing left of me but love.

Despite the challenges, by 1978, I was blessed with two more children, Adnan and Imran, turning our family of three into what felt like my very own cricket team. The ceaseless symphony of cries, bickering, and arguing often made the days feel endless, and my utmost priority became survival and maintaining my sanity. Managing the nineteen-month gap between the two boys proved to be a challenge, as they were both in their early years and demanded a great deal of my time and attention. At times, it felt like I was raising twins, with every task doubled and made even more strenuous.

Thankfully, Qayum was a hands-on, nurturing and attentive father. When he was around, he made sure to assist with nappy changes and the bedtime routine and entertain the children for a few hours. In those precious moments, I would try to catch up on some sleep, take a quick shower, cook a meal, and freeze any extra leftovers for the week. I was constantly tired—a sentiment every new mother understood, internalised and truly empathised with.

To my dismay, Qayum found himself immersed in gruelling, extended work hours, being on call for various branches across Yorkshire. The longer, more strenuous hours left him knackered and unable to assist with the myriad of tasks around the house. On those difficult days, I would tuck my little ones into the pram—Amber, now five, no longer needed one. We made regular visits to our local park. There, the kids could run around freely, escaping the confines of our home.

I also joined the local mum's club, where I managed to meet many wonderful locals. Newfound acquaintances blossomed into a robust support system. One of these was Jenny Shires, who lived just five minutes away from us in Sunningdale. She kindly tended to me when I was sick, brought groceries, and even helped with Amber's school pickups and drop-offs. From carpooling to assisting with errands, these kindred spirits took a hefty weight off my shoulders.

Fifty years later, I remain in touch with these compassionate souls. Looking back, I now fully appreciate the advice my mother once gave me: protect your sisterhood. Unlike the dynamics between men and women, women inherently understand one another, whether as wives, mothers, daughters, sisters, or even friends. The lived experience of a woman is unique, shaped by her own struggles, societal expectations, demands, and even biological realities. The nuances are deeply complex, ones that men, in their simplicity, often cannot fully comprehend.

Part II
Calling and Challenge:
Career, Loss and First Signs of Illness

CHAPTER FIVE

---✦---

WORK LIFE

Moving Forward

In the crisp October of 1979, Qayum's career path led him to the bustling streets of London. Fortunately, he had accepted a transfer to Habib Bank at the Moorgate Branch, which was great news but also meant that we had to be separated temporarily, with the weekend commutes. For six long months, our quest for a home continued until, finally, in the budding spring of 1980, we found our haven.

Our new home came with a vast 130-foot garden, which soon became Qayum's sanctuary. He would lose himself in its expanse, often anchored by London's cultural landmarks and the rush of city life, all while eagerly anticipating his return home.

Yet, despite Qayum's picky nature, his choice of Hillview Gardens proved ideal. Nestled amidst lush pastures, with Headstone Manor on one side and Pinner Park Farms just a stone's throw away, it was a haven of peace and tranquillity. Even after 45 years, I still find solace roaming through these glorious green spaces.

Oh, how no one warned us about the road rage we'd face in London! Qayum would turn into a beast, as if we were in survival mode, cursing at drivers and blaming the city's congestion. Yet, I couldn't help but attribute some of the blame to him for the chokehold the traffic seemed to have on us.

But Qayum's weekends were marred by irritability, moodiness, and seclusion. His reluctance to socialise with people perplexed me. I couldn't fathom leaving him behind while I went to visit friends, bound by the cultural norms imbued in us since childhood. In my culture, it was considered inappropriate for a woman to leave her husband at home while she went out to visit family or friends. It simply wasn't the social norm, and the values I was raised with didn't allow for it. As a result, I never did. This was unheard of. Instead, I would stay behind before the television, with his sulking mood gnawing away at me. He would always have the news on—BBC, ITV, and Pakistani channels— playing continuously in the background. I would sit in the same room, focused on my schoolwork, marking papers, and lesson planning, barely paying attention to the broadcast. Qayum, on the other hand, would offer a constant running commentary on the news. Amidst the noise and chaos, I'd occasionally ask, "What's happened?" to which he'd respond, "Don't you listen?" I couldn't shake the feeling of resentment I felt towards him, a sense of compromise that was directly infringing on my own happiness and free spirit.

Still, Qayum's days were consumed by the arduous task of renovating our new home. With mounting bills, we couldn't afford professional help, so Qayum became a master of all trades. From laying carpets to installing windows, he poured his heart and soul into transforming our house into a comfortable home. It was then I realised the depth of his talents and the extent of his dedication to our family.

Embarking on Teacher Training

In 1982, under Qayum's influence, I enrolled in evening classes for an "Access to Higher Education" course. This was the only path available to me in pursuing a teaching career, as my degree from Pakistan was unfortunately not recognised. After a decade of full-time mothering and raising three little humans, I was ready to step into the workplace and feel useful again. It felt like reviving a dormant, rusty engine in a vintage Maserati that was left unused for years. The engine whined and groaned with the few attempts to start the car—like a person being resuscitated reluctantly back to life. Yet, with persistence, it eventually came to life, eager to hit the road. I hoped my renewed vitality and passion for education would resurface in the same way. The very moment I found myself back in the confines of a classroom, watching students grappling with a question and requiring my assistance, I knew I was going to snap back into motion as though I had never left.

Qayum was a self-made man, and all his true life stories were a great inspiration for me. I was ever so grateful for him encouraging me to go back into education, knowing full well it was the one thing that brought me joy and fulfilment—beyond raising my beautiful children. Qayum graciously took it upon himself to part-time childmind while I went to build mastery and proficiency in both English and Maths. I felt so invigorated, having my mental faculties tempered with the challenges of a mathematical equation or the semantics of an excerpt that I was about to engage and dissect critically. This led me to a four-year

B.Ed. Honours course, which included teacher training at the Polytechnic of North London. The program specifically inspired ethnic minorities to go into further education, ultimately paving the way for a career in teaching.

It was another very taxing time in my life—running a home and raising my kids while studying through the night. So many times, I wanted to quit everything.

However, it was Qayum's words that got me through the difficult days. He'd share the adage: "Rome was not built in a day."

He would also encourage me, with unwavering conviction, by telling me: "I know it is hard, but you can do it!" He would advise me to give up children's swimming, library sessions, and visits to parks, but I could not accept that; as children grow, they may never get that opportunity. So, I tried and continued to be a self-sacrificing mother.

Crossing a Finishing Line

Finally, in the warmth of June 1987, my educational journey culminated in my official appointment as a qualified teacher. My passion for teaching was solidified with a degree, and my teaching was conveniently nestled near my home in Harrow. I was grateful my job was so close, curtailing the long hours commuting that might otherwise be spent with my children.

As the summer term refused to yield, I found myself thrust into the throes of employment with a new supply role at my local school at Uxendon Manor. I was forewarned that it was an extremely challenging class with a rowdy and notorious bunch of pupils; however, I knew I was ready for the challenge.

Yet from the outset, my impostor syndrome came looming over me, my anxiety flowing like a tumultuous wave. Faced with the first-day jitters, akin to starting the first day of primary school, my first blunder began when I accidentally parked in the headteacher's parking space—a fact unbeknownst to me but one that left many staff members enraged. If that weren't enough, I faced another incident in the staffroom, where I had encroached upon the staffroom rules by sitting foolishly in the senior's armchair, thus prompting an immediate reprimand from the staff.

As I settled into the role, the issues persisted with incessant whispers, glares, and murmurs swirling around about my suitability for the role and the perceived mistake of hiring me; however, undeterred by their cynical comments, I was firm, defiant and poised in my self-belief and capabilities. I was determined to manage these unruly pupils with great heart and soul but, more importantly, with rigour and delicate firmness. Fortunately, my pedagogical approach proved effective, as I managed to command the students' attention and respect, which initially felt like a near-impossible task. To the headteacher's astonishment, I finally earned her respect, as well as that of my colleagues. My work, rather than my words and promises, spoke volumes.

Our financial circumstances improved, marking the beginning of a positive trajectory on the home front. My husband assumed the role of a reliable provider, and for me, that entailed finding fulfilment beyond the confines of our home. I found a passion and purpose that extended beyond being a kitchen-bound housewife, which was something I learned was indispensable to my sense of self.

Our improved financial standing meant that we were able to refurbish our home and go on holidays, besides visiting Karachi to see our families. These holidays were more than recreational breaks; they were exciting opportunities for us as a family to bond. We were a tight-knit family and treasured our quality time together wherever we went. In the first few years, we had already visited many cities in Pakistan, England, Europe, the USA and Canada. We embraced the various cultures, languages, and foods and also learned about customs, traditions, and life lessons that no book could teach.

CHAPTER SIX

———✳———

TRAVELS

Umrah

In the early nineties, we managed to check Saudi Arabia off of our bucket list and perform the *Umrah* or lesser *Hajj*. We cherished our time there; the sheer excitement of touching the Kaaba, and especially the Black Stone, several times during the day was heartwarming. As my eyes rested on the Kaaba for the first time, I was completely mesmerised by its beauty and majesty. The sight of it, shining softly in the sunlight, was unlike anything I had ever seen. Qayum and I stood there, overwhelmed, tears silently flowing down our faces. At that moment, words felt insufficient. I was reminded to make dua, and as I looked at the Kaaba, I prayed for Allah to guide me and my family on the right path of Islam. We thanked Allah with full hearts for bringing us to this sacred place.

The children, full of joy, eagerly kissed the Black Stone every time we circled the Kaaba, their excitement filling the air. Located in the eastern corner of the Kaaba is the Black Stone (Al-Hajar al-Aswad), whose now broken pieces are surrounded by a ring of stone and held together by a heavy silver backdrop. According to tradition, this stone was given to Adam on his expulsion from Paradise in order to obtain forgiveness for his sins.

Touching and kissing the black stone is an act of worshipping Allah and a sign of respect. It certainly does not forgive sins; only Allah can forgive sins. It's a rock of Paradise, so it is precious and respected, but it is just a rock, and it does what rocks do; it just sits there. Amid the bustling crowds and the hum of voices, a peaceful calm washed over me. In that chaos, I felt a deep sense of tranquility. It was an experience like no other—exciting, satisfying, and spiritually uplifting. The image of the Kaaba, its beauty and the emotions it stirred is something I will carry with me forever.

Saudi Arabia has changed so much since then. The country has embraced modern technology and has become one of the most advanced in the world. Medina, still the most welcoming place, had grown, with luxurious hotels replacing the simple ones we used to stay in during the 80s. The glamour of both cities had risen, with new attractions like the Palm Tree Farms and Mount Hira Exhibition drawing tourists from all over the world.

I remember my mother's trip there. When she returned, she couldn't stop talking about how much she wanted to go back. At the time, I didn't fully understand why. But now, after my own visits, I realise what she meant. There's something indescribable about that place, something that touches your soul.

I feel incredibly blessed that Allah has allowed me to visit His house more than once. Every visit has been a gift, a chance to reflect, to pray, and to reconnect. The journey is physically exhausting—long walks, crowded spaces, the heat—but the spiritual peace it brings is priceless. It strengthens me in ways words cannot capture, and for that, I am deeply grateful. Nowadays, these moments are considered impossible to replicate. At the time, we may have taken these moments for granted, but as an adult, I have come to appreciate how much my family strove to ensure we were holding onto our faith and remained steadfast. As the children were growing up, we were accustomed to making a pit stop to Umrah as an annual tradition that served as a meaningful way to reconnect with Allah at the holiest site on earth.

Our First Hajj

In 1993, Abdul Qayum and I embarked on our trip to perform our very first Hajj. Qayum had always been reluctant to make this big trip, particularly because he was already struggling to commit to his five daily prayers. At the time, he was grappling with his faith and had other priorities which consumed him. A journey as momentous as Hajj seemed like a distant, far-fetched step to take at the time.

But to my amazement, our visit had a positive ripple effect on Qayum, inspiring a renewed commitment to his five daily prayers. His dedication, although admirable, left Qayum equally irritable with the kid's lack of fervour and spiritual devotion. More often than not, I reminded Qayum of his own shortcomings and prolonged halts, emphasising the gentleness and grace he needed, which the children would now require too.

It became increasingly apparent that Qayum was losing his patience with the kids. There was a growing divide between how he viewed the world and how the children and I saw it. Qayum criticised my style of parenting, accusing me of being too soft and gentle with them.

To him, I wasn't preparing the children for the real world. While I was sheltered, soft, and lenient, he was well-travelled, cultured, schooled, and street-smart, knowing the ways of the world. To him, I was far too naive and forbearing. We'd often bicker, as I'd always advocate for gentle parenting—a principle I'd championed as a teacher. He was receptive at times, but more often than not, he remained obstinate, indifferent and emotionally withdrawn.

Mood Swings

The Harrow community grew, and we began to meet more like-minded couples and families through the mosque. With minimal time and effort, we found ourselves quickly integrated into the Muslim community, particularly with families who had children around the same age as ours. Weekends became a canvas for celebration, a mosaic of gatherings. Many of these new acquaintances, which eventually turned into friendships, were forged through the children's local school, which meant we also attended weekend parties, iftars, and regular social gatherings.

On Christmas day, my home would overflow with at least thirty to forty guests. It wasn't about marking the occasion; rather, it was an opportunity for the children to enjoy the holiday season with their friends. Qayum and the children cherished these occasions, and as for me, I simply loved being a gracious host and seeing all the contagious smiles and positive comments on my culinary skills, as well as the hum of conversations.

But it was not long till a call came that altered the mood of festivities. The disquieting news was that Qayum was admitted to Whitechapel Hospital after suffering a heart attack... The news hit me like a punch in the stomach. His stay spanned a couple of weeks, and upon discharge, he was asked to change his diet, eating only raw vegetables, notably broccoli, cauliflower, peas and beans, all steamed in the microwave while trying his best not to consume sugar. Embracing gardening as a newfound hobby among other chores around the house, Qayum admittedly had more time on his hands. More time to help around, but it also became tiresome and problematic.

After a six-week hiatus and slow recovery, Qayum returned to work, but the man who came back was not the same. A discernible transformation in Qayum's demeanour swept over him and our lives from that day on. A deepening grumpiness that seemed to grow stronger with each passing day. It was an indescribable state, which, over time, left me feeling like I was living with a stranger at times. Qayum and I were disagreeing often over fundamental principles when it came to raising the kids. His rigidity, strictness, and loss of composure meant, more often than not, I was shouldering more stress than less with Qayum around. I tried to excuse his behaviour, blaming it on the medication, knowing these things always came with side effects. However, the truth was that Qayum's mood swings were taking a toll on us all as a family. Agitated, the children would often ask, "What's wrong with dad?" and I would reassure them by saying, "He is just recovering from his heart episode; he'll be fine!"

I embraced a more relaxed parenting approach, trusting that our children would naturally discern right from wrong as they matured, without the need for strict discipline—a departure from my own upbringing. Qayum, however, perceived the world as a perilous place, adopting a more protective and stringent stance. Occasionally, his silent treatment cast a shadow of dissatisfaction over our home; his mere presence at these times conveyed his disappointment in me, a sentiment the children keenly sensed.

These moments of tension infiltrated various aspects of our lives, making it challenging to maintain harmony. Yet, amidst these episodes, there were also periods of understanding and unity that sustained our family's bond.

In 1998, he was offered an early retirement. Qayum took to reading the Quran and Islamic literature, staying informed about current affairs, and engaging in activities such as walking, swimming, cycling, gardening, and household chores. He kept his mind and body active, and he was a great help when I was busy at work. His former interests, like socialising and networking, no longer excited him. Instead, he became irritable and grumpy over minor details around the house, such as whether the towel was not hung properly by the children, if their rooms were untidy, or even if they were mischievous to each other.

Amidst these changes, our family holidays continued as a constant adventure. Life, now markedly distinct from the carefree seventies, unfolded with a happily married daughter, prankish grandchildren and ambitious sons at universities. I was busy with my leadership role at school while Qayum was embracing retirement. Life was more quiet and serene—but certainly not one free from problems.

Qayum had begun to give up on holidays and was increasingly uninterested in my adventures, so he encouraged me to travel with my Muslim workmates and cousin. He seemed content in his cocoon. I went to Morocco with my cousin, and it was a very different experience. I missed my husband constantly. He no longer showed interest in joining me on these trips, and with each passing day, it felt as though he was growing more distant. He wasn't keen on enjoying the resorts, and I had no choice but to make the most of it. Still, I appreciated the independence he gave me and felt truly grateful for the opportunity to travel. I was proud of him because I knew so many people, especially women, who couldn't even leave their homes for a walk, let alone go on holiday.

Despite the ups and downs, I still had the energy and desire to explore other places, and soon a school colleague joined us. Together, the three of us travelled to Prague and Dingle Bay, enjoying short getaways of just two to three nights during the half-term holidays.

I always made sure to leave food for my husband before I left, and I've come to appreciate the truth behind the saying, "The way to a man's heart is through his stomach." In fact, many top chefs would argue that the way to anyone's heart is through their stomach. Qayum, who loved his meals, was the kindest soul. He would always save some food for me when I returned so I didn't have to cook right away. His thoughtfulness meant the world to me, and my affection for him was endless.

Chapter Seven

———— ✦ ————

Loss, and First Signs of Illness

Tragedy Strikes

In the chill of December 2006, Qayum and I embarked once again on a journey of a lifetime—Hajj—with our youngest son, Imran. Little did we know, upon our return in January, we would be struck with the most tragic news any mother could receive: the passing of her child. That winter evening, I had to do the unthinkable—say goodbye to my beloved Imran.

It was sudden, life-altering, and beyond what a parent's heart can endure or explain. Even after all these years, the grief remains sacred ground—too deep for words.

As believers, we accept Allah's divine decree, trusting that His wisdom encompasses all things—even those we cannot understand. In this time of loss we took solace in our faith and the knowledge that Imran was and will be in the mercy of the MOST merciful.

That truth anchored us. We did not understand, but we trusted. From that trust came the strength to keep living, one day at a time.

Some losses can't be told in stories—they live in silence, in prayer, and in the quiet spaces of faith.

Imran was not just a joyful, carefree soul; he was our very own ray of sunshine. Wherever he went, his presence brought warmth, joy and infectious laughter. He had a natural charisma that drew people to him, effortlessly making others feel comfortable in his company. His mere presence brought us endless warmth and endless infectious laughter.

Imran and I shared a special and unbreakable bond—a connection built over years of love, understanding, and sacrifice. When the time came for him to go to university, he made the decision to stay home. He didn't want to venture too far from home; he cherished our post-supper conversations and my channa masalas, niharis and biryanis far too much. This meant the world to me, as it would to any mother, mainly since Amber had already settled into married life in America since 1998 and Adnan, my middle child, was deeply immersed in his studies, his mind constantly engaged in the pursuit of knowledge. Medicine was not just a career choice for him, it was a calling—one that demanded his complete dedication. With an insatiable curiosity and relentless determination he embraced the challenges of his field, often disappearing into a world of textbooks and late night revisions.

The words *Inna lillahi wa inna ilayhi raji'un*—surely to Allah we belong, and to Him, we will all return—became our daily mantra. We repeated these words to comfort our aching hearts, reminding ourselves of Allah's decree, the inevitability of mortality, and the certainty of our final return to Him. Losing Imran cast us into a dark space so profound it felt almost impenetrable. We were adrift in a sea of perpetual grief—our eyes teary and our tongues tied, struggling to grapple with the words to convey the incomprehensible pain we felt. We withdrew into ourselves, neglecting our own well-being in the process. I felt deserted, and almost everything in my life, was suspended in time. I longed for my parents, wishing they were alive to comfort me during these testing times. All I craved were their soothing words, tender touch, unwavering support and unconditional love.

As I grappled with the pain and grief, I remembered a time when I was newly married, in my second week or so, staying with my in-laws in Karachi. My sister-in-law casually remarked on my exuberant nature, colourful outfits and party-going habits, deeming them inappropriate given our mother-in-law was grieving the loss of her daughter—who had passed away 12 years prior.

At the time, I couldn't fully comprehend the magnitude of her words in my untested state. It wasn't until I faced the same tribulation that I began to comprehend the depths of her gnawing grief and enduring pain. It made me reflect on how words, no matter how wise, are bereft of meaning or value when they fall upon an innocent soul shielded from pain and suffering. Words, like seeds, may scatter and settle, lying dormant until life's storms awaken them. With time and experience, their meanings shift and evolve, taking on new forms as they merge with our growing understanding. Yet, in the moment they are spoken, there exists a chasm—a disconnect between the speaker's intention and the listener's capacity to truly comprehend.

Losing a parent is akin to losing one's past, but to lose a child is to lose one's future. Losing a child is the hardest experience anyone can endure. It certainly shakes every parent to its core.

Parents and children are the scaffolding of generational labour that upholds a family and gives it life and meaning. The adage that time is a healer was far from the truth. No time could ever heal this insurmountable pain, for grief becomes a part of you, dwelling in you. But ultimately, this is the price of love—it is accepting that your love remains, but it may not always be around. To love, especially anything that is mortal and transient, is to grieve. Thus, to grieve is not a sign of weakness or a lack of faith, just the price of love.

With the love and understanding of Qayum and my unwavering commitment to my faith, first and foremost, I was able to slowly garner strength and patience. I was so fortunate to have a loving and caring husband who devoted himself to me, fully with his groundedness, tenderness and kindness. He constantly reminded me of Allah's wisdom and plan. As the Quran instructed, I comforted myself with prayer and patience, fully acknowledging that only Allah could hear my pain and give me solace and comfort.

More often than not, the notion of patience is misconstrued. Patience is seen as someone who is stoic and experiences pain silently. However, true patience is, in fact, experiencing the depths of your pain, despair and trauma while simultaneously believing that Allah's plan is the best of plans. It is trusting His decree and accepting that pain is an integral part of that experience.

A beautiful quote from Yasmin Mogahed's book, *Healing the Emptiness* states: "The idea that emotion and crying are signs of weakness is absolutely false. It is not a weakness, nor is it an oversight in God's design. It is a mercy. Therefore, to deny this natural part of healing is very harmful. If we deny our tears, we stall the healing process. We get in the way of our own healing. This is the divine design of Allah. He gave us tears as a mercy and a cleanse. It is part of the healing process."

This was liberating to read, for it highlighted the humanness and mercy in our religion. In my Asian culture, there is often a cautionary sentiment about shedding tears in case it nullifies the sin. It was drilled into us that being faithful meant suppressing emotions and never conveying helplessness and pain. However, not only are these emotions unavoidable, but they actually serve as a pathway to attaining nearness to Allah.

The Echoes of Absence

In the midst of Imran's untimely departure, Qayum and I retreated into our shells, engulfed by deep sorrow and grief. Our home became a cocoon—dark yet comforting, shielding us from the outside world. In the stillness, we found an unspoken solace, a shared understanding, as we sought refuge in each other's broken spirit. Even our children, bound by the same grief, joined the silence. It was as though the house itself mourned with us, its quiet corners echoing with the weight of our silence.

Yet, as time wore on, I found myself haunted by this silence. Only a select few dared to pierce the deafening void: those who cherished Imran offered gentle whispers of remembrance. Even now, eighteen years later, the memory of Imran wavers like a candle flame, casting a gentle glow over our cherished memory of him. Their remembrance, though limited, was a soothing balm for my aching soul—a testament to the enduring power of love channelled through grief.

To my children, I cannot help but extend my deepest apologies for neglecting myself and them in the process and for forgetting that they were equally in pain. Lost in the labyrinth of my own grief, I failed to see beyond myself. I failed to attend to them when they needed my comfort, strength and guidance. I failed to offer them the solace they so desperately required. Yet, I trust in their compassion and understanding that, despite being their mother who has always been selflessly devoted to them, I was a grieving mother who couldn't do anything besides try to survive another day.

It was only fifteen years later while attending a bereavement course on how to become a bereavement home visitor that I knew this was my way of garnering the strength and courage to navigate my own pain while supporting other grieving people. It was only then that I learned the importance of understanding that grief wasn't singular—that there were also my children who had lost their precious brother. There was nothing I could do to take away my children's pain besides asking Allah for forgiveness and the strength to be present for my children while I live.

Unsettling Hints

In the winter of 2009, we travelled to Malaysia in search of solace and a respite from our pain and grief. Our destination, Kuala Lumpur, was exciting and held the promise of distraction. One evening, after a day spent exploring the city, I found myself standing beneath the soft glow of a street lamp. From a distance, I could see the route back to the hotel. It was within sight, but Qayum steered us towards a longer, more strenuous route against my wishes. The humidity pressed down on me, the air heavy and oppressive. We walked for what felt like an eternity. Exhausted and frustrated, we eventually made it back to the hotel in one piece.

That night, I lay awake, feeling powerless, bewildered and confused by what had transpired. My thoughts churned: how could Qayum behave in such a stubborn and hurtful manner? Was he angry with me? I had no answers.

Upon our return to London, I confided in our children about the unsettling encounter, expecting them to reassure me and dismiss my worries. Instead, they expressed concern and immediately urged their father to seek medical advice. He was, of course, reluctant and convinced he was fine. To me, he was always infallible—a paragon of knowledge and capability. He could be nothing short of incredible.

However, as time passed, subtle signs began to emerge, hinting at a shift in Qayum's clarity of thought. Initially dismissed as insignificant quirks in his personality, these moments seeded confusion in our home, escalating into silent conflicts. It often fell to me to lighten the mood, and I didn't hesitate to weave playful jests into our conversations. In Urdu, I would usually say: "*Satya Gaye ho kya?*"—"Have you gone cranky?" is a phrase that, without humour, might have only fuelled more tension. Yet, despite my efforts, unease lingered. Qayum's phlegmatic nature, once so admirable, now seemed perplexing. I found myself wondering: was he incredibly strong and resilient, or simply ignorant and blase?

It wasn't until a heated argument erupted—over a missing sum of money—that it became undeniably clear something was grievously wrong. The accusation of pilfering from Qayum's wallet was an indelible scar that was etched in my soul from that day on. That day marked a pivotal moment in our marriage, a turning point that felt like an irreparable, unsalvageable fracture.

Hours of arguments, stretching endlessly, passed before the truth finally emerged: the money, supposedly missing, had been spent on various situations he had forgotten amid the whirlwind of daily affairs.

Relief came, yet the lingering doubt instilled in Qayum through his words and look of complete distrust in me was a feeling I could never shake. How could the man I loved and trusted the most harbour such suspicion? This was the same man who, without hesitation, had given me access to a joint bank account when we married in the early seventies—an unquestioning trust, an extraordinary gesture for any Asian man. From the beginning, Qayum had made me feel we were a team. He had given me the freedom to spend from the very first day I came to the UK.

As Qayum's memory faltered and accusations came more easily, I grappled with a sense of helplessness, isolation and anger. At times, I found myself questioning the essence of our bond. Yet amid the doubt and pent-up anger, I sought solace in our most treasured memories, comforting myself with the belief that perhaps marriage—and love—naturally had its ebbs and flows its highs and lows.

Rising to the Challenge

Every day unfolded predictably despite being on the brink of living my long-awaited dream. For twenty-two years, I poured my heart and soul into my job at a school in Harrow, nurturing hopes of reaching the summit and becoming a head teacher. Yet, it felt like an elusive mirage, obscured by the fabric on my head—a simple cloth that expressed my faith but seemed to stand as an unseen barrier on my path. In moments of doubt and despair amidst the noise of the world, I held tightly to a quiet conviction: my path to Him was the only path that truly mattered.

When I decided to blow the whistle on the unfolding events at my school, an unexpected opportunity arose. I was offered the role of acting head teacher at my Harrow school, a stepping stone to a permanent head teacher post at Ayesha Community

School, an Islamic institution. It felt as though Allah had reserved the perfect role for me—one that allowed me to thrive without compromising my faith and values.

In the tender embrace of Qayum's love, I found solace amid relentless waves of grief. His understanding ran deep, enveloping my life-long sorrow with unwavering care. His constant reminders and words of affirmation were like sturdy scaffolding, supporting the fragile walls of my inner temple—a temple that sometimes wavered and weakened but one he knew how to mend and fortify. His presence became a refuge, a blanket for my weary soul. In those profoundly intimate moments, I truly understood the verse that likens spouses to garments for one another. Just as a garment drapes the body, offering unmatched closeness, so too did Qayum's solace and understanding envelope my soul.

It was Qayum who spotted the advertisement for the head teacher position, a flyer I had carelessly discarded. He found it at Regents Park Mosque and, recognising its potential, encouraged me to apply. His unwavering faith in me pushed me toward this golden opportunity.

Through the challenges orchestrated by Allah, we refused to succumb to despair, persisting in our faith without wavering. Though I considered myself deeply committed to my faith, it was often tested. I constantly reminded myself that calamities are invitations from Allah to draw nearer to Him. Each adversity was not just a trial but an opportunity to practice patience and gratitude. Amidst despair and anguish, I drew comfort from the timeless wisdom of Ibn Al-Jawzi: "If this dunya was not a station of tests, it would not be filled with sickness and filth. If life was not about hardship, then the prophets and the pious would have lived the most comfortable lives."

From our teachings, we learn that trials are woven into the

fabric of earthly existence. Our books of history are laden with truth, bearing witness to the myriad of trials faced by our revered prophets and messengers: Adam's expulsion from Paradise, Nuh's heartbreak over his son's defiance, Ibrahim's test of fire and sacrifice, Yaqub's tears of longing and blindness, Musa's confrontation with the tyrant Fir'aun, and Prophet Muhammad's (peace be upon them all) year of sorrow, with the loss of his wife Khadijah (RA) and uncle, Abu Talib.

In the solitude of my thoughts, tears streamed down my cheeks relentlessly. Whether I was cocooned in the solitude of my car or beneath the deluge of my shower's embrace, tears flowed unabated, like an ever-present companion. With every tear, I turned to Allah, entrusting my suffering to His Divine wisdom and seeking solace in His promise of beautiful patience. Imran, our precious blessing, was bestowed upon us by Allah's grace, and it was by His Divine wisdom that He chose to reclaim him. While I grieved openly, Qayum found solace in reciting the Quran, reading Islamic literature, immersing himself in newspapers, walking in nature, gardening, and cherishing camaraderie with his Jumuah friends. His quiet strength became my beacon of hope, illuminating a path forward even through our shared sorrow.

Fortunately, my role as a headteacher became a mercy from Allah—a respite and a precious gift for which I remain eternally grateful.

Waiting at the Gate

In April 2010, three years after losing our gem, Imran, Qayum agreed to accompany me for Umrah once again. We visited the holiest site on earth, seeking the patience to heal and move forward fully.

We turned to the words of Allah in the Quran when He says:

"Seek help through steadfast patience and prayer;
for observe, God is with those who patiently
persevere."

....
(Surah Al Baqarah, 2:153)

Whenever we visited Allah's house—a sanctuary for every Muslim—it welcomed all, regardless of their walk of life: whether the person was a fully-fledged sinner seeking repentance, a new Muslim or someone like myself, grieving and yearning for solace in the form of a warm blanket for my weary soul.

Before each visit, we carefully arranged a meeting point, aware of the sheer magnitude of the place. With millions of people converging from around the world, the chances of losing one another were high.

Yet, on one occasion, a couple of mishaps occurred, leaving me unfairly blamed for not being at the correct gate at Haram Sharif, the Noble Sanctuary—a term Muslims revere when referring to the holy sites and their surrounding areas. The grandeur of the Kaaba, with its two hundred and ten gates, often overwhelms even the most seasoned visitors.

I had been waiting diligently at the designated gate, yet Qayum failed to show up. What troubled me most was that he knew this gate extremely well—we had been here many times before. As minutes stretched into hours, confusion clouded my thoughts. How could Qayum, with his razor-sharp memory, forget something so familiar?

Eventually, we reunited at the hotel. My energy was far too depleted to argue with Qayum, which I chalked up to a mindless error. Still, I couldn't ignore the gnawing question: what happened to my vibrant Qayum, whose remarkable superpower was his intelligence and exceptional memory?

The Qayum I knew—witty and full of life—seemed to be fading. I was feeling as though I could no longer forge a connection with him, for I was communicating with an empty vessel of a shell. I began to entertain the notion that his cognitive abilities were declining reluctantly, and perhaps it was time to let go of the man he once was. This realisation ushered in a new grief. It wasn't the sudden loss of a loved one but the slow erosion of a person—the gradual vanishing of the cherished traits that had once made him whole. And with those parts of him, pieces of me felt lost too.

Upon our return to London, I immersed myself in my job, filled with excitement for the work ahead. While I was busy, Qayum remained home-bound, though never without purpose.

He kept himself occupied with chores around the house, executing them with precision and grace. His passion for gardening flourished as he dedicated so much time and patience to his plants, eagerly anticipating their bloom. Beyond the garden, his insatiable thirst for knowledge drove him to delve into books on world politics, history and current affairs. The Quran was never far from his reach; he practised Arabic and memorised verses, reciting them in his prayers with unwavering devotion.

Qayum's pursuits extended beyond our home. The streets of Harrow became his second domain, where he cycled and walked daily. Yet, when the evening sun dipped below the horizon, he often chose the warmth of home and the companionship of his wife over that of his friends—a quiet reminder of the bond we shared, even as his brilliance dimmed.

Headship and Politics

Over time, I became increasingly busy with my headship, especially given that the school was underfunded. This proved quite challenging, as I had never worked in an Islamic organisation before, and I had been warned that such environments were often rife with politics and tension. Despite these challenges, I loved my job. I would leave home around 7:15 am to avoid the traffic and wouldn't return until 6 pm in the evening.

I was fortunate to have a husband with many hobbies and skills. He kept busy with cycling, walking, reading Islamic literature, the Qur'an, and newspapers. Since his retirement in 1998, he also began waking up for *Tahajjud*, the Night Prayer. This is a voluntary prayer performed by Muslims. While it's not one of the five obligatory prayers, it's highly regarded for its ability to strengthen spirituality, patience, perspective, and inner strength of character.

I began to notice irregularities when I came home early or on weekends. The curtains would be drawn in the afternoon, and he would sit in front of the television, watching the same news channels repeatedly. Feeling unsettled, I would often ask him, "Don't you get bored?"

Over time, I learned to be agreeable and refrain from voicing my opinion. For example, when we went to Tesco, he would comment that everything looked different and the store had been rearranged. I would simply agree, saying that perhaps the supermarket had changed its shelving and product placement even though I knew nothing had been shuffled and the layout was exactly the same.

Reckless Driving

Qayum's driving had become increasingly erratic and unsettling. My only *cha-cha* (my father's youngest brother, Taher Memon) lived in Stanwell near Heathrow, and we visited him frequently. Qayum, always eager to take the wheel, displayed impatience, recklessness and an inexplicable anger towards other drivers. As a hijabi, I couldn't help but feel deeply embarrassed. I gently reminded him of the importance of embodying our faith by being gentle, composed and respectful on the road, adhering to traffic rules. But my words seemed to fall on deaf ears.

Despite my pleas, his driving remained reckless—like a rollercoaster ride. I often felt nauseous and unsettled, repeatedly reminding him of my vertigo and how fragile I felt.

On the other hand, Qayum had always possessed an impeccable sense of direction. He confidently navigated routes without ever needing a GPS, relying on his own knowledge. However, there was a particular time that stuck with me. As we approached a familiar right turn towards Staines, Qayum decided to go straight instead of turning right. I repeatedly told him he was going the wrong way, but Qayum, who never trusted my navigation skills, brushed off my concerns. This was the first time he had ever gotten lost.

We didn't use any navigation systems, as we never needed them. Qayum was his own SAT-nav, believing that modern technological tools only served to make people lazy. Despite his reckless driving, he had never been in an accident—just a couple of speeding tickets here and there.

That evening, as we were returning home, something far more alarming happened. Qayum stopped right in the middle of a roundabout, blocking access for other drivers. Horns blared furiously as he sat there, confused and unyielding, convinced he was in the right as he pointed to a red traffic light in another direction.

That was the last day Qayum drove a car.

My son, Adnan, had to step in despite the numerous altercations with his father. Who was Adnan, to tell his father never to sit behind a wheel again? But he knew it was the right decision to protect his father and others on the road, even if it meant playing the bad cop. For Qayum, losing his independence was incredibly difficult, and he was upset for months, but we all remained true to our word. The situation with Qayum was difficult as he was getting increasingly absent-minded. He often retorted and denied my words, even when they were encouraging and kind. It wasn't just his mental deterioration that was difficult to witness; it was the unsettling transformation of his personality. On the road, he became monstrous and volatile, unable to see the lethal consequences of his driving.

Secretly, there were times when I wanted to report him to the DVLA to suspend his licence, but I couldn't bear to hurt him. He cherished driving, as he dearly held onto his licence card from the early sixties. On our trips to my uncle's place, he would often make grand declarations that things had changed— the library was new, for instance, even though the route and area were so familiar, and nothing had really shifted at all.

Part III
It's Alzheimer's

CHAPTER EIGHT

---✦---

DESCENT AND DEVOTION:
ALZHEIMER'S ONSET

A Blessed Day

I t was that time of year when autumn erupted into shades of burnt orange, pastels and varying hues of brown. I absolutely love this season. One afternoon, I returned home eager to enjoy my cinnamon latte and relax while taking in the view of my garden. Having finished my conference early, I seized the opportunity to go for a walk—something I had always treasured as part of my holistic, therapeutic routine. That Friday remains vivid in my memory.

When I walked through the door, I found Qayum deeply absorbed in a newspaper, which was unusual. It was a Friday, a blessed day, and Qayum was always strictly devoted to his prayers on Fridays. But that day, he seemed distant. He explained that he had tried to go to the mosque only to be turned away by the guard. He was infuriated and couldn't understand why the mosque guard had not allowed him to enter. His favourite meal—lamb shanks cooked in *Shaan*'s Nihari Masala—remained untouched, which struck me as strange.

Qayum insisted that he had left at the usual time, 7:30 am. When I gently suggested that the guard may not have let him in because it was too early, he grew irritable and convinced me otherwise. He even mentioned that he asked people on the street what day it was, and they confirmed it was indeed Friday. I had so many questions, including whether his friend Mahmood was there, but Qayum wasn't making sense. As his agitation mounted, I called Mahmood, who confirmed that Qayum had indeed been standing at the gates but was denied entry.

Friday was Qayum's favourite day—the day of congregational prayer, a day of blessing and renewal—a tradition and ritual for every practising Muslim family. Every week, he would meet up with a close family friend, Mahmood Kayani, and they would travel on the Metropolitan line from North Harrow to the Regents Park mosque, also known as the Central Mosque in London.

They were part of a group of six friends—brothers in Islam, family friends—who gathered there to pray, chat, and share their lives. This group, later named the Jummah Group, still exists today. The group grew and soon included all of us wives. The men realised that incorporating food into their meetings added a new dimension to their gatherings, as Fridays alone didn't provide enough time for socialising.

Our first gathering took place at Rayners Lane, hosted by Brother Tameez, and featured delicious Afghani kebabs. Most of the attendees were able to make it, and it was soon decided that we would host these meals at our homes once a month. Qayum truly cherished these get-togethers, enjoying both the company and the food—especially the selection of desserts.

Over time, like with anything, the group evolved with new members joining. We lost some people to old age, and others faced new challenges and illnesses. As for me, I chose to step back after Qayum's passing; it became too difficult to participate without Qayum by my side.

That afternoon, I decided against a walk and instead lay awake grappling with the realisation that my husband was not okay and slowly deteriorating. I knew something was amiss; how could someone so familiar with the routine of going to the mosque for years arrive at the wrong time and emphatically deny it? The clocks were definitely unchanged.

My mind raced with a thousand thoughts. It felt ominous— like the clearest sign of the disease Qayum was about to endure. I couldn't hold back the tears. As a woman who had already endured the loss of her father's sight, his battle with prostate cancer, the sudden death of her mother, the unexpected loss of two close friends, and the heart-wrenching death of her beloved child, I had learned the only way to cope was to trust in Allah.

That night, as torrents of rain lashed against the windows and the sky felt darker than ever, I lay awake, consumed by worry. A gnawing thought took root within me—I felt it in my bones— something was deeply wrong. This wasn't the Qayum I knew. The Qayum, who always arrived punctually every prayer, now believed he was on time but was convinced that the guards had barred him entry out of sheer malice, The clock hadn't changed yet, so what was happening? My mind raced with endless questions, all leading to the same harrowing realisation: I was losing him.

This incident was the clearest indication yet of a dreadful disease afflicting Qayum. Whether it was a brain tumour or something even more insidious, I didn't know. In my heart, I prayed for strength and fortitude to face whatever lay ahead. I clung tightly to Allah's promise:

> *"Verily with every hardship comes ease."*
>
> **(Quran 94:60)**

With every pang in my chest, I reminded myself of Allah's mercy. From a young age, I had been taught that life is a series of trials meant to strengthen us. Each test is uniquely tailored, and its purpose is known only to Allah.

We learn from the stories of our prophets, who endured severe trials: Prophet Adam, who was expelled from Paradise, and Prophet Moses, who confronted Pharaoh and led his people through the Exodus. Prophet Yusuf was betrayed by his brothers, sold into slavery and wrongfully imprisoned. And Prophet Ayyub, who faced severe illness, the loss of wealth, and the death of his children. Yet, in every story, Allah's mercy and wisdom prevailed.

The stories of the Prophets in the Quran, who endured severe trials, gave me strength and hope. Their God is my God too. Prophet Ayyub, who, despite losing everything—his health, his wealth and his children—continued to call to Allah with unwavering faith. The townspeople ridiculed him and attributed his calamities to his sins, and yet he remained optimistic and hopeful in Allah.

This world may judge harshly, but I held on to the hope and mercy of Allah. I knew that with Allah, I could get through anything. I trusted that no matter how heavy the trials, my heart would find solace in His remembrance.

Following Qayum's glaucoma surgery and the distressing incident at the mosque, it became clear that he was struggling.

There was a noticeable decline in his memory, visuospatial skills, language abilities, executive functions, and orientation. This decline seemed to coincide with an episode of angina earlier that year when he had also been rushed to hospital. In response, Qayum was referred to a neurologist at the memory clinic for evaluation.

Trials in Every Scripture

Scriptures across different faiths emphasise the significance of trials as a fundamental part of our human existence. In Christianity, it is stated, "God ordains tests for us, not for His sake, but for ours." These tests are intended to build and fortify our character, as mentioned in James 1:2–4. In Judaism, trials are viewed as a gift, a spiritual elevation and a means of drawing closer to God. They are a way of finding completeness.

Amidst the challenges of caring for Qayum, I found solace in gratitude. I immersed myself in daily gratitude, reflecting on my numerous blessings—my faith, my health, my financial stability, and the many genuine, close-knit relationships I had developed. Confronting adversity, coupled with gratitude for everything one endures in life, is crucial for enhancing self-esteem, and I can vouch for this from personal experience.

Above all, I took pride in being by Qayum's side, finding peace amidst life's many trials. Each day passed with struggle, but despite how overwhelming and difficult some days were, I knew I had to stay resilient—Qayum was relying on me now. As a woman who had weathered the storms of life—from my father's blindness, his prostate cancer, and the sudden death of my mother to the unexpected loss of my son—I recognised my inner strength and resilience.

After the loss of a child, the depths of sorrow reach an

unimaginable peak—beyond which no greater pain can exist. The indescribable pain shattered me, leaving my heart completely broken. Yet somehow, through this immense suffering, I developed an unexplainable strength and courage to endure even deeper pains. Now, faced with Qayum's health struggles, I had to summon the strength to navigate a new reality. A reality that required me to find sources of strength that fortified me spiritually, physically, emotionally and mentally. The strength that was needed not only for Qayum but also for myself, my children, family, friends, and the future.

Health Warnings

Alhamdulillah (praise be to Allah), life had settled into a rhythm that worked for both of us. My days were filled with ample hustle and hard work to make ACS a successful school despite the numerous obstacles placed before me as head. Somehow, I managed to persevere without sinking into depression or grief. At home, Qayum seemed relaxed, and I always felt Allah's presence in my life, knowing that everything I did was for His sake alone.

However, Qayum was slowly deteriorating, and his illness became increasingly evident. Despite his blood pressure readings and the extensive list of medications he was compiling, he remained active. He had received some IT training at Harrow College in 2000, right after his retirement, and was proficient with technology and current world news, making him well-versed in current affairs.

At times, I suspected Qayum's illnesses—glaucoma, voice loss, prostate issues, and memory decline—as simply part of the ageing process rather than anything more serious. Despite these challenges, Qayum remained strong-willed and resilient. He would make solo trips to the hospital, not wanting to trouble anyone, even for severe conditions such as having a stent put into his heart. I would pick him up afterwards and see the confidence and independence he carried, with or without me. Life was tough, but somehow, I found the strength to persevere. He never liked to burden anyone with his issues, and at times, I couldn't help but wonder whether his strength was truly rooted in his faith or if he was merely putting on a front due to his pride. I leaned toward the former, given his frequent reminder that we can only depend on Allah and no one else.

On a bitterly cold winter day in 2012, Qayum began losing his voice. My immediate fear was cancer. We went through voice therapy to help him regain his speech, and fortunately, he was able to speak again. However, I noticed a significant decline in his short-term memory. He began misplacing items like his keys, wallet and legal documents more frequently, forgetting important appointments, and falling into a monotonous routine, stuck in a repetitive cycle. This decline, however, had its advantages: he would quickly forget stressful situations, which meant he failed to hold on to unwanted grudges.

Qayum had always struggled with a sensitive stomach. Initially, the stomach issues seemed minor, but they gradually developed into something more serious, leading him to undergo endoscopies in 2011 and 2012. We suspected aspirin might be causing a chronic inflammatory disorder in his sinuses and lungs, but after visiting Northwick Park Hospital, he was diagnosed with angina pectoris. This came as a surprise, as Qayum had never faced any chest pains. He remained positive, reminding himself that his condition was not life-threatening.

While Qayum was homebound, I began noticing some unhealthy habits. He developed regular sugar cravings and an increased intake of sweets, often hiding a tin of chocolates under the stairs. He had a deep love for desserts, sometimes skipping meals entirely to indulge in puddings and bars of chocolates. His sweet tooth was a generational trait inherited from his mother. It became somewhat infamous, and everyone knew about it. He always joked that he had a special pouch in his tummy where he stored all his sweets. It was uncontrollable, and I had to keep telling him to stop.

Qayum always wanted to see me happy and content. He knew we couldn't change our reality, only our perception of it. After performing Umrah, we realised the only way to cope with life's challenges was through faith and patience. Our faith grew stronger each day, though mine often wavered. Qayum would remind me that everything is by the will of Allah and that we must accept it—even though his heart was heavy as he spoke these words. He carried my pain, too. I couldn't help but feel that age-related illnesses, which are expected as the immune system weakens, are manageable. But unexpected illnesses come as a shock and test us in ways we can't anticipate.

I tried to heed his advice and reflect, but the pain of losing Imran, my precious gem, cast a dark shadow over our lives. The thought of living without him made us despair. Still, we chose to plod along with heavy hearts, feeling lifeless and drained. We would reflect on one another's losses, reminding ourselves that this life is fragile, transitory, and unpredictable. The only consolation I had was the reminder that Allah knows best in His infinite wisdom, as He is Al-Alim (The All-Knowing).

Despite the challenges, I felt a deep connection to God. I knew I was not alone and was reminded of the miraculous power of gratitude.

"Gratitude is from a high station—meaning a rank or level. It is higher than patience, asceticism and fear. Why? Because all these stations are not required for themselves but a means to an end, a bridge to something else. Whereas gratitude is a destination in itself."

I reflected on the countless blessings Allah had bestowed upon me—blessings that many could only dream of: a loving and supportive husband, beautiful, intelligent, and healthy children, good health, a family, friends, a home, a fulfilling job, and lush green surroundings for my daily walks.

An Unusual Situation

It became increasingly unsettling when Qayum's memory issues led him to share ludicrous falsehoods about me and my family. He began telling his friends that he had been forcibly married to me and that my father had orchestrated the entire thing. It was strange for him to say something so far from the truth. Our marriage was arranged, but culturally, my father would never intervene in such a callous manner.

The absurdity of it all made me laugh heartily, though I would later reprimand him privately, reminding him that my father had never come to London and would never do such a thing. Qayum would jokingly disagree, insisting that my father had indeed come to London and demanded that the matter remain a secret. While this situation seemed amusing on the surface, I found it deeply disrespectful.

When I shared the situation with my friends, they laughed at my expense. Even the psychologist found it amusing, and none of us realised that it was the beginning of a more sinister disease.

At the same time, Qayum would often repeat the same story about his arrival in the UK in 1959—how a friend had helped pay for his airline ticket, his accommodation in Bedford Square, his two jobs, and how he supported his family back home.

Despite hearing the story repeatedly, it started to irritate me. His persistent retelling, combined with his growing memory loss, began to wear on my nerves.

Assessment Time

Finally, the much-awaited day arrived for Qayum's appointment with Dr. C. J. Mummery at Northwick Park Hospital. I approached the situation with blind optimism, unaware of what lay ahead. Dr. Mummery, a gentle and approachable woman, met with us for less than 15 minutes. She recommended an MRI scan, explaining that it was the only way to uncover what was happening with Qayum's brain activity. Of course, this is extremely distressing for anyone.

Fortunately, the MRI was scheduled for exactly one month later at the same hospital, which wasn't too far away. We would need to take the bus to get there, a journey I wasn't accustomed to, as I usually preferred walking to most places.

Over the next few months, there were numerous appointments, including several assessments, which ultimately led to a referral by our GP to Dr Dullith De Silva, a psychiatrist at the Harrow Mental Health Trust's Bentley House. This also required a bus ride, which only added to my growing frustration as I had to take time off work for these visits. In hindsight, I realised how much I had taken for granted—the little blessings in life, such as Qayum sitting behind the steering wheel and driving us to appointments.

Qayum, however, knew the bus routes well and guided us to the hospital, navigating the changes with ease. This period marked the beginning of numerous assessments, which eventually led to Dr. D. De S's referral. Once again, the trip required another bus ride, contributing to my increasing exhaustion from taking time off work to attend all these appointments.

Qayum had always loved walking, and I often accompanied him on strolls. He still ventured out alone, but I began to notice troubling changes. He refused to hold my hand when crossing streets and instead attempted to stop oncoming traffic with his walking stick, putting us both at risk. His irritation and resentment toward drivers, as evidenced by his shaking the stick at them, was out of character and deeply concerning.

An occupational therapist from the community mental health team arranged a home visit to assess Qayum's road safety skills. While he demonstrated a satisfactory ability to cross roads safely, I knew something was fundamentally wrong. He saw no error in his behaviour, continuing his walks around Harrow and the farm where we lived and remaining active at home by cleaning, vacuuming, disposing of the rubbish, managing the heating, and even changing light bulbs. I missed his DIY skills, especially his gardening, which we both cherished. Every evening, he would make me coffee, and I would leave him small tasks to complete at his convenience. Despite everything, we thanked Allah together each day.

Qayum's behaviour became increasingly erratic. He refused to give me the door and car keys, opened the door to strangers, and engaged in odd activities, such as hiding items around the house. This is when I had to invest in an alarm system for our home.

On the 21st of May 2014, the psychologist wrote to the GP clinic and provided the following results:

On cognition, he scored 16/18

On memory: 6/26

On fluency: 8/14

On language: 17/26
On visuospatial skill: 14/16
With an overall score of 61/100
And on another mental examination, he scored 22/30

The conclusion was clear: Qayum's memory was in decline. Qayum spoke nearly eight languages of the Indian subcontinent: Bengali, Gujarati, Hindi, Kutchi, Punjabi, Pustho, Urdu, and, of course, English. His language skills remained relatively fluent until 2017. However, most of his language-related brain activity was likely occurring in the left side of his brain, which was still functioning well. He spoke in Gujarati to the psychologist at the memory clinic and in Punjabi to the builders next door. While this was impressive, eventually, all his thoughts became jumbled, and his speech turned to gibberish. Still, Qayum managed to communicate confidently, making it difficult for anyone to refute his words.

Our next consultation was at the Neurology department at the National Hospital, Queen Square, in London, on Monday, 30 June 2014. We went for a neuropsychological assessment, unaware of the emotional rollercoaster that lay ahead—a living nightmare, a daily battle of denial, shock, and anguish.

At the start of the journey, I pleaded with Allah, feeling vulnerable and weak, saying I am only human, with a heart the size of a fist and burdens amounting to what felt like a mammoth of a mountain. I suspected a malignant brain tumour or something more sinister. Whatever it was going to be, I knew it was something that would test me and push my comfort zone to its maximum.

I felt an overwhelming sense of internal peace as I begged Allah to keep me firm in my beliefs. I sought comfort in seeing other people's hardships and struggles, and in turn, I would be grateful to Allah for all the blessings He had bestowed upon me. I would console myself with the story of Prophet Ayyub, who was tested with illness, loss of wealth, and children—not to mention people's ridicule and judgement as they attributed his trials to his sins. And yet, Prophet Ayyub still thanked Allah and showed immense gratitude.

And so, in the depths of despair and immense struggle, I reminded myself of Prophet Ayyub's life, a parable and a lesson to remain patient in the face of all circumstances. I knew Allah would reward me for my patience and goodwill.

CHAPTER NINE

MEMORY LOSS

It's Alzheimer's

On the 14th of July 2014, our lives were irrevocably changed. The doctors at Northwick Park Hospital announced, "It's Alzheimer's." The doctor showed me the scan images and confirmed the diagnosis. No further explanation was needed; the weight of those words was enough to silence us both for the next hour.

In a daze, I turned to Google to learn more about the disease, opening myself up to a flood of health scares and horror stories. I learned then that Alzheimer's is the most common cause of irreversible dementia in adults, progressing gradually from mild forgetfulness to total disability. It involves the structural and chemical changes in the brain, causing long-term impairment that no current medication could reverse or halt. The doctors were unable to reassure us; there were only drugs that could mitigate the symptoms to help manage behaviour and emotional responses, making it somewhat easier for the carer to cope.

What did I know about Alzheimer's before this moment? Nothing at all. The only thing I knew at that moment was that my life was about to change forever, and Qayum was going to need me by his side for this long, dark, and uncertain journey.

There is a verse in the Quran that says:

"Verily with every hardship comes ease."
....
(Quran 94:60)

There must have been a reason why this verse was repeated twice in Surah Al-Inshirah. It is meant to reassure us, to remind us to stay strong. I had full conviction that Allah would reward me for my patience and inner resolve.

When Alzheimer's came knocking unexpectedly, I felt an immense sense of anxiety; however, it also brought me closer to Allah and taught me about the illness itself and the many ways it affects people's lives. I constantly reminded myself of the verse from Surah Al-Baqarah, verse 286: "Allah does not burden a soul more than it can bear."

After Qayum's diagnosis, I made sure to conduct extensive research into this malignant and lesser-known disease. Many people in my community, including family, close friends, and acquaintances, were unaware of Alzheimer's and its ramifications. I couldn't blame them, as it was less known compared to conditions like heart attacks, strokes, and cancers. These diseases often have visible effects that leave people physically unwell and attract sympathy. I carried out extensive research, joined the Alzheimer's Society, and held on to the hope that one day, this brutal disease would be cured.

Abdul Qayum had never forgotten anything in all the years we had been together, including our wedding in 1972. I was always bemused by his perfect memory and astounding mind. So, any changes at first seemed insignificant and unalarming. Qayum remained calm, and he had no issues with his forgetfulness, attributing it to his age. Bemused, I would ask him whether he was really that sharp and forgot nothing. I considered him extremely lucky, given that I was nearing menopause and forgetting a lot of things.

I remember vividly the day I drove the children to school. As we were nearing the traffic lights, I asked, "Where are we headed?" They thought I was joking and teased me about my forgetfulness. At the ticket machine, I found myself staring blankly. I was at the underground station, heading to an appointment, and at the counter, I was staring blankly, not knowing where I was going. The station master noticed my confusion and kindly suggested I buy a ticket and just hop on. He reassured me in jest, saying it would come to me, and sure enough, it did—before I reached the next station. These moments of forgetfulness were becoming a part of my daily life.

In Search of Qayum

Qayum's habit of walking regularly was incredibly beneficial, even as the early stages of his diagnosis progressed. Initially, he managed well, wandering around familiar streets and areas until he found his way home. But then, one day, he didn't return on time. It was the most terrifying experience of my life.

Frantic and overtaken by worry, I jumped into the car and searched for Qayum in every corner of Harrow—East, West, North, and South. Once I had explored every area, I called the police, explaining that my elderly husband, who had Alzheimer's, was missing.

Fortunately, the police arrived within minutes. While I was pacing back and forth in my living room, overwhelmed with anxiety, the officers tried to calm my nerves with light-hearted jokes as they searched through every closet and cupboard. I remember one officer even asking to borrow one of Qayum's suits after seeing the vast array of options he had. Qayum's suits hung beautifully in his wardrobe, a testament to his pride in keeping his things immaculate and in perfect condition. He always took great care of his belongings.

I was upset with myself, wishing I had done more to ensure the safety of my husband. I had taken precautions by placing pieces of paper with Qayum's name, address, and our home phone number in his wallet and coat pockets in case he found himself in a situation where he couldn't find his way home. This was something I had learned from my father, may Allah rest his soul in peace, who did the same for my mother after she began to forget things following a stroke. When my father passed away in 1996, I found all the notes delicately placed in his drawer, a poignant reminder of his care for her despite his own partial blindness. Of all the grand romantic gestures, for me, this was the ultimate labour of love—silent, unwavering, and deeply soulful.

The police asked for a full description of Qayum's features and clothing, but in my panic, I struggled to recall the details. Eventually, I managed to provide a good enough description, and soon, his image was circulating on Twitter with the headline, "MISSING FROM HARROW."

I had a strong feeling, a sixth sense that Qayum was on the bus he often took. It was route 183 from Pinner, which continued to Golders Green, a journey of more than an hour.

I shared this with the police, hoping it would make their search significantly easier.

After what felt like an eternity of waiting—though it was, in fact, six long, agonising hours—the police found Qayum. The very next day, I ordered a GPS smart tracker for my dear husband. I couldn't fathom the idea of losing him again. The pressure was overwhelming, the strain intolerable, and the tension unimaginable. With every worst-case scenario playing through my head, I catastrophized and lamented what was yet to come.

Navigating the System

My journey began with a referral from my GP to support agencies, such as Harrow Carers and Milman Resource Centre. It started with a few sessions on dementia with a lovely lady named Gill. On my first day, I was asked what I would do if I were given a day off from my caring role. I replied, "I came to learn how to look after my husband, not myself." This moment was crucial, as Gill followed by giving me a detailed breakdown of a caregiver's journey and what to expect.

She warned me about the challenges of living with a family member suffering from dementia, including how it transforms family relationships—physically and psychologically. Initially, I didn't fully understand the weight of those words until I lived through eight relentless years of this journey.

Alzheimer's Research states the following in their document "Dementia in the Family: The impact on carers".

Caring for a family member with dementia:

• Is challenging: carers manage difficult changes in their loved ones' behaviour and personality, including aggression in some cases. Caring full-time can leave family members feeling socially isolated and having to meet hidden costs.

• Is rewarding: caring is often a very rewarding experience that can strengthen family bonds through the close and intimate relationship shared.

• Can change family relationships: changes in behaviour and personality can cause family carers to treat their loved one in a different, more childlike way. Carers' relationships with siblings can also become strained as the amount of care increases.

• Impacts psychological and physical health: the negative health consequences of looking after a family member with dementia are well documented.

Laughter: The Best Medicine

On April 17, 2014, after our first appointment with Dr. C. J. Mummery at the neurology clinic in Northwick Park Hospital, I was blissfully unaware of what lay ahead. Immediately after the appointment, we headed to Harrow shopping centre in the relentless rain, which was pouring down in sheets, accompanied by gusty winds. Our umbrellas flapped wildly as we struggled to get them back in place. My headscarf clung to every inch of my skin, turning it into every modest hijabi's living nightmare. As we made our way to the local bank, I noticed it was open unusually late. I asked, "Why is the bank open at this time?" Qayum, with a cheeky smile, replied, "It's Christmas!" We both laughed in unison. It was a moment of pure joy, a moment of bliss, completely oblivious to the anxious and unsettling thoughts that often crept into my mind from dawn till dusk—and sometimes even through the night.

Despite the seriousness of Qayum's condition, his humour always shone through. The bank was hosting a mortgage evening for its loyal customers, and though it was summer, the air was crisp and biting, with a sharp and unforgiving wind. Such moments of confusion and irony left us sharing a secret little laugh, providing a much-needed respite from the constant strain of life—a strain that became a companion we couldn't escape.

Throughout my life, I have always believed in the adage "laughter is the best medicine," and it became an indispensable outlet for us during our journey with Alzheimer's. Every night, when I couldn't sleep, I would use the quiet hours to write poems—often humorous musings on life's absurdities and joys. Absurdities that, if I didn't cry about them, I had to laugh about to take the edge off. I had always written funny poems for my colleagues' farewell parties at school, and now, amid this journey with Qayum, it seemed like the right time to do so once more.

Despite Qayum's memory loss
We treasured our laughter a lot
We had a good laugh together
Sometimes not knowing what?
Laughter is contagious and it spreads
We felt better when we laughed
It took away the blues
It gave us both the feeling of a boosted mood
A rise in adrenaline that was good
Something to be treasured
Without a measure
Gold of pleasure
Was our subtle leisure, our laughter together

The Dreaded News

After much waiting, on August 7, 2015, we met with Dr. Mummery. She showed us Qayum's MRI scans, revealing that his brain had shrunk—confirming the diagnosis of Alzheimer's. The news was absolutely devastating, but in my naivety, my immediate question was: what does this mean? The simple reply was: memory loss. She showed the scan images to highlight the extent of the brain damage, and oh, I was unprepared for what I was about to discover. While I could come to terms with the memory loss and forgetfulness aspects of the disease—having seen many elderly people with similar issues—I had no idea of the full implications of this disease.

The brain damage was gradual, and the effects were not immediately visible. The disease felt like a drip-feed process, as things only got gradually worse in dribs and drabs. Qayum's behaviour was strange, yet he seemed unaffected, which, in a numbingly soothing way, made it easier to cope. He appeared well, smartly dressed, and sociable, yet behavioural issues were emerging. This was the first sign that things were not as unaffected as they had seemed. Any tasks that involved thinking, talking, dreaming, or walking—all actions dependent on brain cell communication—were being disrupted by Alzheimer's disease.

I distinctly remember the early days when Qayum would cut into long queues at shops, causing outrage among other customers. Earnestly, I always tried to explain his dementia and assure people that he meant no harm, but we were met with dirty looks and disparaging comments. This was deeply discouraging and hurtful, not only for my husband, who was battling a merciless neurodegenerative disease that was eroding the very essence of his identity but also for me, who was mourning the loss of the love of my life—a loss greater than death, I would argue.

This, coupled with the stark reality that my life was undergoing a 180-degree alteration, was overwhelming. My husband was no longer the protector guarding his herd. I was now the carer, wife, mother, father, and protector of our home, and I needed all the strength I could muster. I understood that each case of Alzheimer's was unique, which made it a challenge for health professionals to provide clear guidance or set expectations from the outset. I also understood that healthcare providers were in a difficult position; they couldn't overpromise and underdeliver, making an already sensitive and painful time for a grieving family even more strenuous.

Given the lack of information, I considered it a blessing, holding tightly to strands of hope that my husband might make a recovery or that the extent of his deterioration could either be halted or postponed. But damn, I was blissfully unaware of the fact that I was about to watch my lifelong companion wither away, slipping away forever, right before my eyes. August 7, 2014, is a date etched in my memory as a turning point in my life—a day that marked tragedy, the sands of time slipping through the hourglass as I watched my husband's time with me slowly ebb away.

From Headteacher to Carer

My role shifted from headteacher to carer very quickly. It was not something I had time to transition into, but something I needed to accept and acclimatise to in a heartbeat. Not for a moment did I feel resentment or a lack of gratitude for what that meant for me. Instead, I was filled with immense gratitude for Qayum, especially the last 42 years spent under his care and protection. I valued his unwavering commitment to me from the moment he said, "I do" to embarking on and journeying through life with him, away from my hometown, my family and friends. It was a no-brainer that I would happily give up my career to care for him and make it my life's mission to make him my top priority.

I had full faith in my Creator that He was going to ease my journey by giving me the strength to cope. With my faith, I also believe that life doesn't happen without its share of sadness, fear and grief. These were inevitable in life, and no one could escape any of these trials except with the will of Allah.

In Surah Al-Baqarah, verses 155–157, Allah (SWT) says:

> *"And we will surely test you with something of fear and hunger, loss of wealth, lives and fruits, but give good tidings to As-Sabirin (the patient). Who, when afflicted with calamity, says: 'Truly, to Allah we belong and truly, to Him we shall return.' They are those on whom are the Salawat (i.e., who are blessed and will be forgiven) from their Lord, and (they are those who) receive His mercy, and it is they who are the guided ones."*

Knowing that Allah tests his believers with trials and tests increased my conviction that I was simply being tested, and it didn't take away from His love and mercy. I was reminded that it was simply the work of the devil to make me question my faith, and it was my responsibility to empower my mind with positive self-talk. I searched for duas (supplication) and came across one that Prophet Ayyub had called out to Allah in times of hardship. He called out to Allah:

*"Indeed adversity has touched me and you are
the most Merciful of the merciful."*

I was always reminded of Surah Qaf, verse 16 when Allah says:

*"And we have already created man and know
what his soul whispers to him. And we are closer
to him than his jugular vein."*

I now had no choice except to trust Allah fully as I had always done, but now I had conviction of His promise. All I needed to do was to speak to Allah and feel His mercy and tranquillity envelop me.

"Allah will be enough for those who trust Him."

(Quran 65:2-3)

I quickly learned that calling out to Allah was the essence of prayer. The connection can be strengthened by regular remembrance and recitation of His Ninety-Nine names. I tried to learn them by heart so I could use Allah's names as part of cultivating my faith and making each one of my prayers even more sacred, unique and personalised. Each name embodies a different feeling and mood, depending on the event, crisis and situation. I always loved using the names Al-Latif (The Gentle), Al-Wakeel (The Trustee), Al-Fattah (The Opener) and Al-Razzaq (The Provider). The names provided me with hope and conciliation that Allah alone will look after me in times of difficulty. Invoking His name in the shadowy stillness of the night, forehead resting on the prayer mat in prostration, brought moments of serenity no person could ever steal or take away, even amidst life's greatest difficulties. Tears streaming and heart aching, my cries of desperation gave way to an unexpected stillness and calm the moment I lifted my head and rose from the ground.

Qayum was undoubtedly beginning to feel the brunt of this cruel disease, and I found myself increasingly anxious and bewildered by his behaviour. It was particularly strange when, at 2am and, at times, 4am, he would insist on going to the bank. He was fully suited and booted and ready to go out of the door, and I had to explain every time that it was too early. Dementia was wreaking havoc on his internal clock, especially on his sleeping schedule, waking and meal times, which most of us take for granted. His behaviour, although mindless and not deliberate, became obnoxious and infuriating. I was left helpless, struggling to tame many angry situations that escalated very quickly into rage and insistence to go to work.

I vividly recall the deep sense of helplessness and despair I felt in those moments. It was like being in a tunnel that was only getting increasingly claustrophobic and dark, and I was trapped inside. Without the support and formal caregiving training, I constantly felt like an impostor, not equipped to look after my husband. It was the overwhelming anxiety of a new mother, caring for a child who seemed so fragile, delicate and alien-like. Any wrong step and a surge of fear would follow, as her sole mission was to protect them from the world.

Watching Qayum, once a pillar of tenacity and stability to the family, now gripped by confusion and disorientation was heartbreaking. The disease had not only stolen his precious memories but the very rhythm and routine of our lives. Each night was met with uncertainty as he roamed around the house. I was reminded of his condition and how his illness was only progressively getting worse. It was as if we were both trapped in a matrix, ruled by a malevolent entity—an unforgiving disease that was orchestrating our lives, dragging us down an abyss of darkness and chaos.

After some extensive reading about the dreaded disease, I decided to blog on the ALZ Society website. I decided to write about the symptoms patients face, such as illusions, delusions and hallucinations. Additionally, I wrote about the struggles faced by caregivers, particularly in communicating with patients whose verbal skills are impaired by the disease and the inevitable burnout that follows.

Some of the things that were happening to Qayum were scary and happening quickly, like his onset of delusions, escalating confusion, hallucinations and sundowning, among a host of other side effects. I learned that sundowning was characterised by late-day behavioural changes that included disorientation and restlessness, which could be best avoided by keeping rooms bright before dark, thereby prompting a reset to the circadian rhythm and tricking the person into thinking it was still daytime. There was also research to suggest that finding diversions could help with the onset of late-day anxiety, and what better than our cat Mau, who was a balm to the soul? Every evening, I would usher Mau to Qayum's lap, where Qayum would routinely stroke and comfort him. Remarkably, Mau would sit on his lap, facing him as though he understood Qayum was unwell. Cats are incredibly sensitive and pick up on energy. Whenever I was feeling sad, Mau would huddle beside me or on my lap and try to comfort me. I would instinctively look away, unable to bear the sadness in his eyes as he saw me so upset.

As Qayum's Alzheimer's progressed, I utilised the opportunity to work on building our relationship. I did my best to adapt to his daily changes and routines, so I am available to him as an anchor and a robust pillar of strength. He never expressed his needs or took advantage of his situation to exploit me. Instead, he chose to silently suffer alone. It was for this reason that I chose to develop an internal schedule that worked for both of us, which meant I still had my cat naps, but I was equally available for him when he needed me. This looked different every day, and my sacrifice and adaptability were a must for life to go on. I had to pick my battles carefully.

I continually renewed my intentions and reminded myself that being of service to my husband was the highest form of worship and devotion to God. I began to see pleasure in choosing to care for him, for in my care for him, Allah was pleased with me and enveloping me with His care and mercy. It was like making deposits into my spiritual bank, ensuring that on the Day of Judgement, when I will be in need of Allah's mercy and forgiveness for my shortcomings, there will be enough goodness to serve as a form of salvation and testify on my behalf.

Memory Gaps

Qayum's symptoms got progressively worse, and the demands for caregiving intensified. The added burden of sun downing meant there was increased confusion and agitation, which intensified in the late afternoon and evening, and I needed to consider more serious measures to manage his symptoms. In the hope of alleviating his discomfort, I invested in a specialised light designed to improve sleep and combat Seasonal Affective Disorder (SAD). While the light therapy eased his nerves, it didn't improve his condition. Companies claimed that such therapy could help regulate sleep cycles in dementia patients, although the evidence was inconclusive, and more large-scale trials were needed. Every attempt to seek therapeutic routes was counterproductive, as he frequently tried to close the lights. Instead, I would find Qayum high on energy, meticulously tidying his drawers, sometimes until the early hours, which meant he remained awake all night. Most nights were extremely difficult; I just wanted to rest, but I reminded myself that this was one of Qayum's self-soothing habits, and I couldn't take it away from him.

There were frequent episodes of important items going missing, whether it was the house keys or my nailmcutter. If I questioned him, all hell broke loose around the house, and his anxiety would intensify. I often felt cornered and intimidated as Qayum would refuse to cooperate, and I would be left searching for miscellaneous items for hours. To mitigate this, I began hiding items like the house keys in a room that was inaccessible to him, but this wasn't always successful, as all his free time led him to rediscover some of his old cherished possessions like his first UK driving licence, an Islamic book he had co-authored in the sixties and his first passport. Those discoveries, although seemingly arbitrary, prompted me to believe that Qayum was trying to reignite some of his treasured memories from the past. Although he did not articulate this to me, I was able to put the pieces together.

Through the journey, I began to heartily accept that Qayum was not being obnoxious or irritable, but as I was witnessing from his MRI scans, his brain tissues were damaged. While things were deteriorating for Qayum, my role was transformed dramatically from a headteacher with a structured routine that kept me sane and productive to a caregiver who was struggling with uncertainty and unpredictability. Initially, I found myself anxiously searching and trying to find answers on every available platform—but eventually, I came to understand that health was not a one-size-fits-all solution, and lived experience and information gathered from the net were two entirely separate realities. The learning was continuous, and I needed to trust my intuition in a lot of the moments. As a carer, I found myself overwhelmed by the relentless strain of being a caregiver rather than his disease per se, and I struggled to find enough support groups for the caregivers who were giving up everything for their loved ones.

There were no Admiral nurses either for advice at the time due to a shortage of funds; these are similar to McMillan cancer nurses. They specialise in dementia care, working with families and people affected by dementia. They help people manage complex needs, provide tailored clinical advice and psychological support and advise people about financial issues and benefits. I am certain this would have been very beneficial if there was someone to talk to.

When the days got tougher, I was reminded of the words of Prophet Muhammad (ﷺ), who said:

> *"The extent of the reward will be in accordance with the extent of the trial. Allah tries us, and whoever is content will have contentment, and whoever is angry will have anger." (Tirmidhi)*

These words reminded me that our trials were temporary and only there to strengthen us and bring us closer to Allah. Despite making regular prayers for Qayum's full recovery, I recognised the futility of such a request and the need to redirect my prayers towards seeking ample strength, patience and wisdom. I began reciting a specific supplication, which eventually became a habit in the nineties:

"O Ever-Living, O Self-Subsisting, by Your Mercy I seek (Your) assistance, rectify for me all my affairs and do not give me charge of myself, even for a blink of an eye."

This was a powerful reminder that even in my loneliest moments, Allah would never abandon me.

In addition to my spiritual endeavours, I turned to a homoeopathic doctor, Dr. Caffoor, near Stanwell to tackle my anxiety-inducing allergies. Although Qayum showed a slight improvement in some aspects, such as drawing a clock, his memory continued to deteriorate over time. The treatments suggested included learning about the remedial properties of coconut oil, such as its ketone production, anti-inflammatory properties, and antioxidants, which I had always appreciated and kept in my pantry, even before Qayum was diagnosed with dementia. However, in Qayum's case, unfortunately, it did not significantly halt or improve his symptoms. Eventually, long drives to the clinic were too strenuous for him, and we had to terminate the treatments.

The journey of caregiving, with all its challenges and emotional upheaval, became a testament to my resilience and faith in God—but also a testament to my love for my dear husband. Despite the difficult days and months, in Qayum, I saw the man whom I had vowed to love unconditionally and unapologetically.

Qayum somehow remembered his name, date of birth and address for a few years into the illness, but on the other side, his long-term memory had gone away completely and was very muddled, though it is assumed that it stays until the very end, but this was not the case with my dear husband as his long term memory had also vanished right at the beginning. Some of the things he would say and do were becoming scary, and very soon, I had learnt new vocabulary like illusions, hallucinations, delusions, sundowning and many more.

CHAPTER TEN

---♦---

SELF-CARE

Fraying at the Edges

I was reading ample reports that shed light on the reality of dementia and the impact it has on family members. One report that stood out was "Dementia in the family: the impact on carers", which underscores the daily realities faced by many of the 700,000 people in the UK who are in this role. Many of the results showed that dementia often leads to social isolation, and the carer would face both health and financial struggles. All too often, carers sacrifice their own well-being to ensure their loved one receives the best care possible. Their experiences reveal the crucial need for research to intervene and make breakthroughs possible.

Milman Resource Centre had organised a lecture by Angela Sherman, the creator of "Care to Be Different", who shared her poignant story of her dad's Vascular Dementia. She described the agony she had endured watching him slowly fade away to the relentless and draining process of trying to claim NHS funding.

When I came across her story, it hadn't hit me as I was still at the beginning of understanding dementia and Alzheimer's. Like many others, I still convinced myself it was nothing more than memory loss. For hours, I would find myself researching this dreaded disease and only becoming more and more fearful and alone. But ultimately, I knew I needed to equally care for myself in this process if I wanted to adequately care for Qayum.

Respite Time

Harrow Carers was literally seven minutes' walk from my home, but I never knew it existed. I attended some sessions on dementia and joined a free yoga class for carers twice a week, where I met other carers who were in a similar situation to me. They provided a range of activities, including yoga, pilates, dance, cooking, and sewing classes, all of which were available free of charge for carers. There were also outings on the agenda.

I loved the yoga and deep breathing sessions, which helped me relax; of course, I soon couldn't leave Qayum alone for fear that he would open the door.

The Harrow Carers got in touch to help with his caring for my respite in October 2016. The head of services came along for an assessment, and I introduced him to two lovely ladies, Hasu and Chandrika. Of course, I had to pay for their services.

In the beginning, Qayum hated every minute of it, and I had to be strong to leave not only Qayum but my whole home with them, but we soon realised that they were professional, trained carers; they would chatter with him in Gujarati and Hindi, give him drinks, watch TV, take him for a short walk and literally keep an eye on him.

I felt it was a Godsend; good people are rare to find these days, and I was so very fortunate, so I started to use the services to go for walks, Quran classes, library, grocery shopping, appointments, coffee mornings, knitting club, even weddings and parties plus attending dementia training. I also joined the carers' group from my GP surgery. These were gifts of respite from my Lord, and I could not deny it.

I was reminded again and again by professionals that I had to take care of myself, or I could be very ill. Living with Alzheimer's required constant engagement, and of course, if I fell ill, then Qayum would suffer. It was a risk I could not afford to take.

On the advice of professionals, I learned to embrace my own company, develop my own interests and hobbies, and, most importantly, fill my own cup. I joined a local knitting club and began crochet as a new hobby. I joined a calligraphy class, but as I was under so much stress, my fingers, hands, and brain just couldn't master it. I visited the local library, where I would find myself immersed in a new book every time, craving peace and quiet. I had a PT trainer, joined a coffee group and attended Quran classes on a weekly basis. These activities helped ease the relentless pressure of caring for Qayum twenty-four hours, seven days a week, allowing me to mentally and emotionally recharge my batteries.

However, it wasn't long until I lost interest in these hobbies as the worry and guilt over Qayum took over me. My social life naturally suffered, and I learned to accept it, but each day became increasingly difficult. Just changing Qayum's clothes was a heavy way to begin the day, and sometimes I felt I was on the brink of a nervous breakdown as he wouldn't listen to me. Some days, I would crawl straight back into bed and just cry out of despair, feeling like an absolute failure. Yet, Qayum's full dependence on me drove me to get out of bed. I had to; I had no other choice.

As life got tougher, I couldn't help but wonder whether I had sinned or was simply being punished. I would try hard to push back on those thoughts and comfort myself with the reminder that Allah was not displeased with me. Instead, He was pushing me to reach my potential, and only He knew my limitations and what I could handle. Allah says in the Quran, and the Hadith confirms it, providing relief to my anxious mind:

"Allah does not lay a responsibility on anyone beyond His capacity."

....

(Quran 2:286)

Tawakkul, or trust, is not merely trusting ourselves that everything will be okay, but believing that Allah is in control. To have faith in Him always, knowing He will look after us. This was my daily cognitive rewiring—literally talking to Allah and asking him to make my days easier and to help me cope in the best way possible. I believed I was doing my best for Qayum, keeping him clean, cooking for his changing diet and palate and taking him on walks. Like motherhood and having a newborn, everything revolved around his needs.

Faith Beyond Memory

Qayum's prayer patterns were changing, and I couldn't ignore his profound devotion to his faith. With all the struggles he was facing, I knew he needed the spiritual fulfilment of prayer more than anything. Determined to help, I spent hours surfing the internet, attempting to find the simplest demonstration of prayer for Qayum to see and follow. After much searching, I found a straightforward and visually guided video on YouTube titled: "How to Perform Salaah." Masha' Allah, I was so proud of

Qayum, who quickly began praying his core prayers five times a day and finding peace in the routine.

I could see how prayer, the most cherished deed for a believer, became a bedrock of Qayum's daily life. Eventually, he was unable to manage longer trips to London for the Friday congregational prayer with his friends—a weekly commitment that he never missed, but which he equally considered a personal highlight. We began attending our local mosque, The Sri Lankan Muslim Cultural Centre of Harrow, which I assumed would make life easier and more manageable. However, within weeks, it became overwhelming. Qayum frequently misplaced his shoes, walking stick and spectacles, continually denying he had moved them. In fact, he went as far as accusing me of imagining things or, for want of a better word, gaslighting me into believing I was the one misplacing his things and that I was beginning to have memory issues. This led to comical situations, such as him opting for misfit shoes that were not even appropriate for the occasion.

As a firm believer in divine intervention, I held on to my patience by a thread. The mosque volunteers and attendants began to see they needed to keep an eye on Qayum, escorting him to a chair in the prayer hall. However, he would refuse to stay seated in one place and would often wander off, causing distress to mosque attendees who simply just wanted to pray and leave the mosque in peace.

By September 2018, I decided to withdraw Qayum's commitment to the Jummah group. I was feeling extremely overwhelmed by the WhatsApp messages and knew the group's rules pertaining to punctuality were going to be difficult to manage. I was tearful, unable to dress Qayum and make an appointment in time. Punctuality had always been something I prided myself on having, but this new reality was extremely disheartening and left me feeling extremely hopeless. Several friends commented that he seemed just fine, which I learned to accept as being the case. It was easier to just be agreeable and smile along sometimes. It was all shallow pleasantries, hollow words, half-hearted enquiries and nothing more. There was no space for vulnerability, encompassing soul-searching discussions or moments of authentic connection; for that reason, I found myself drifting away further and further, retreating into my own space and mind.

Qayum would refuse to listen or follow any instructions, leaving me on the verge of implosion. To ease the burden somewhat, I requested for his friends to take turns visiting Qayum, as I knew his social interactions were very important to him. Sadly, not a single person came to visit. To this day, I couldn't figure out whether it was out of fear of Alzheimer's and not knowing what to expect or a way of protecting their own mental health. Allah knows best. Only three friends called Qayum regularly, to check in, but only Asad Omar, may Allah rest his soul in peace and reward him tremendously, visited Qayum every Eid and occasionally in between. Abdul Qayum cherished every visit, which left me only wishing he visited more frequently. Despite his speech declining, he still managed to form coherent sentences that enabled him to articulate himself and connect with others. Mahmood Kayani, his Jummah prayer buddy, also cared for him deeply, engaging him in politics, world news and spiritual matters. He also helped me occasionally when I needed it. He passed away before Qayum with illness. May he rest in peace.

Qayum was truly blessed and gifted in the way he retained his intelligence even as Alzheimer's worsened. It was becoming increasingly isolating for both of us as Qayum's health was deteriorating, but I knew my Lord was with me at every step. Alhamdulillah, worshipping Allah was second nature to me; I knew it was incumbent upon me to do it if I wanted any blessings in my day.

The Opening

Qayum was unsettled by the idea of joining Milman Day Centre. Seeing others in visible decline was simply too confronting, and I couldn't force him to stay. He was still articulate, aware, and fiercely holding on to his independence. For him, agreeing to stay felt like surrendering too soon—a quiet betrayal of the autonomy he still cherished. And for me, pressing the issue would have felt like a quiet disloyalty to the man he still believed himself to be.

The carers were so helpful and took him for daily walks, giving me time to recharge my batteries. It felt like the early years of motherhood all over again, but harder, for it was not observing the growth of a baby but witnessing the degeneration and withering away of another soul over time. All the care and service weren't about helping Qayum feel better or recover; it was the opposite. It was a painful process of watching your loved one inch closer to their deathbed, preparing for a day of collective mourning for the family. We didn't attend any scheduled sessions at Milman Centre, but when a new centre called The Bridge opened near Harrow Leisure Centre, I seized the opportunity to take Qayum there regularly.

Qayum was apprehensive about going, but this time, I told him it was for me, not him. I needed to find it in myself to return to my social activities and hobbies. I knew by looking after myself first, I would, in turn, feel re-energised to continue looking after him better. Qayum decided to sulk and refused to listen or follow instructions for the chair exercises. On rare occasions, he recognised and named two fruits on a picture sheet. I knew he was giving the carers a really hard time. I knew that I enjoyed the singing, especially the song "*Que Sera, Sera* (Whatever Will Be, Will Be)." However, I began to feel my health was suffering from lack of sleep, and I was developing anxiety. I couldn't turn to anyone who I felt understood Alzheimer's, and why would they? One sleepless evening, an event I was now accustomed to since my husband was diagnosed with Alzheimer's, I found myself writing a poem, one that I eventually showed the carers at The Bridge Centre. I found it so cathartic to write and express myself, and they found it so moving and terribly poignant.

Alzheimer's

How cruel are you,
Just unimaginable
Characteristics have you,
Not only taken memory,
But the whole person, too.
Never heard of you before,
You have taken my husband's life,
Along with mine, like nothing else matters to you.
You seem to have crept in with a vengeance,
So slow and so cruel.
How could you take?
His memory and sanity away,
Leaving him helpless to stay?
My husband seems to be withering away,
His brain all tangled today.
With your cruelty and harshness, we somehow stay.

Why did you knock at our door?
I hate you more and more.
What an intelligent man he was!
A son, my husband, a father, a brother,
A friend, a gardener, a DIY man,
A living Sat Nav and a banker was he.
A master of all trades,
He was amazing and smashing.
Not the same man today
That I knew before you came his way.
You, Alzheimer's, have robbed
Him of his relations
And everything he used to be.
It's absolutely shocking.
In his own home,
He does not know he owns it.
You have left him to a very puzzled life,
Just to struggle and barely survive.
His wife, children, grandchildren,
He does not know anymore.
What can I say about his relations and friends?
He used to adore them, though he loves them all,
But they confuse him even more.
You are responsible
For his limited world.
Television gives him hallucinations,
Sunsets give him illusions.
He feels worried with delusions,
He is frightened and nervous.
What have you done?
No one understands him,

For folks out there know nothing.
He looks smart, so they bombard him with
suggestions.
I hate you, Alzheimer's, for your contributions.
Retirement is to enjoy and relax,
Not to have tears and fears.
But you have robbed me and my dear husband

Of our prime retirement years.
I have heard they are after you, Alzheimer's,
But that's going to be too late
For him and me, too.
All I pray to God
Is to keep you away
From me and all my loved ones.
I hate you, Alzheimer's,
I hate you.
Wish you would just go away.

The Beauty of Trusting Allah

I always knew my five daily prayers were necessary for my soul, yet with time, I began to feel my energy dwindling away. What was once a soul-boosting activity turned into a chore amongst the many others I had to get through each day. The lack of sleep and constant stress had shattered the solid seven- to eight-hour sleep routine I had previously established. The fatigue was building up, and I ignored my symptoms. Five years into Alzheimer's, I felt I had sacrificed everything in my life except for my prayers and supplications. Even in these acts of worship, I would have regular intermissions, pleading with Allah to forgive me. I would whisper as I hurriedly broke my prayers to tend to Qayum. I didn't know whether he was in danger in the kitchen, had fallen, or was hallucinating and imagining people in the lounge or at the door.

Each day, I prayed and did my best to apply my wisdom and turn to Allah's guidance precisely in those moments of supplication. His wisdom, direction, acceptance, courage and immense mercy were always there. I begged sincerely for guidance, and in return, I received the blessing of making the correct decision. One practice that really helped was giving to charity. I noticed the spiritual relief and the Divine mercy I would feel afterwards. From a young age, this act of giving in charity was instilled in us, and I noticed almost instantly the blessings and openings my parents would experience in their life and marriage.

The huge transition in my life, forced upon me, was something I had to not only accept but learn to appreciate. With my background in education, whether in teaching or leadership roles, I have always welcomed and adapted to the inconstancy of people and situations. I never relied on anything staying the same, but I could always rely on the constancy of Allah and the foundations of my faith. I could also see that the more I turned to Allah, the more He fuelled me with strength, clarity, and wisdom, despite all the tears, worry, and fears of the unknown that no one else could comprehend. But I knew that making dua for ease was my only option.

When I look into the mirror, I no longer see myself. I look and tell myself that I have failed to live up to my name, Atiya, which means "gift". I strongly felt like I could no longer do it all. I had to step down and take care of myself first. With all life's changes, simply accepting them and letting them be was life's secret to happiness. Calling out to Allah, knowing He was always there for me.

The Quran says,

"(Prophet ﷺ), if My servants ask you about Me, I am near. I respond to those who call Me, and believe in Me, so that they may be guided."

....
(Quran, 2:186)

Despising change when it is irreversible is futile. Embracing it as the new norm, with the understanding that Allah knows the wisdom behind it, brings peace. With trust in Allah and true *tawakkul* comes a belief that Allah will take care of you, even when things don't go as planned. I vented all my frustrations to Allah through *salat* and *dhikr*, trying to stay calm and collected while everything was sorted. The closer I felt to Allah, the more I felt emotionally and mentally taken care of. I began truly understanding that Allah does things we cannot, and His promise of reward awaits us for our patience. Faith, as I began to understand, was not simply a matter of the heart, a spiritual or silent state, but an active and warm relationship between man and God.

"Patience is bitter, but its fruit is sweet."
Jean-Jacques Rousseau

And as Jalaluddin Rumi says,

"Patience is not sitting and waiting. It is foreseeing. It is looking at the thorn and seeing the rose, looking at the night and seeing the day. Lovers are patient and know that the moon needs time to become full."

What good could come out of Alzheimer's? Yet, the Quran tells us,

> *"And be patient. Surely, Allah is with those who are patient."*
>
> ....
>
> **(Quran, 8:46)**

One Jummah day, I had no energy to dress Qayum or take him to the mosque. Exhaustion consumed me, and I knew I didn't have it in me to take him. Thankfully, he had forgotten it was Friday, but the guilt was overwhelming, as it marked the beginning of no more Friday prayers for Qayum.

Visiting a friend for condolences, I mentioned my struggle with taking Qayum to the mosque. The next day, her brother Ruman and brother-in-law kindly offered to take Qayum to the mosque and keep an eye out for him. This gesture was a tremendous relief, a testament to the kindness and righteousness that Allah rewards. Amazingly, Qayum was patient and content waiting with me at the gates, eager to perform his Friday prayers. Allah's mercy was evident, rewarding my patience as promised.

Despite the exhaustion, I was ready to do everything for my dear husband. Walking twice a day and watching his favourite news channels, *Judge Judy*, somehow became his favourite, with him enduring *Titanic* four times in six months. This routine included giving him showers, dressing him in the best clothes, taking him shopping, and visiting parks regularly. For the first time in our married life, I prioritised things which I had never done before, like buying clothes for him; Qayum loved it.

Rather than focusing on the drudgery of my daily tasks, I began to appreciate his intelligence, personality, and cleanliness, and I thanked Allah for the blessing of such a man. I knew these qualities were rare to find in a man, but I had all of these in my man, even while suffering from dementia. The thought of placing Qayum in a nursing home was unforgivable, despite my children's suggestions. They were worried about my welfare. Deep down, I knew this was unacceptable, not only culturally but also morally and ethically. In most South Asian, Arab, and Muslim households, children pride themselves in caring for their parents until the very end, and this includes any family member or spouse. It was not only a fear of community judgement that stopped me, but also a judgement and self-loathing I would have for myself if I ever committed such an atrocious, selfish, and foolish act. My cultural upbringing dictated that I had a responsibility of care towards my husband in sickness and health. No pious wife would abandon her husband to suffer.

One evening, overwhelmed, I wrote a poem titled *Reaching My Limits*:

Tonight, I feel I have reached the cliff
Of a beautiful mountain
I really don't know how this has happened
When I look around,
I see there is no escape.
All I can do is jump.
Looking below is the deep blue sea.
If I jump, I drown.
I cannot go down
I am tired, I am exhausted.
I feel worn out.
Standing up high on this cliff
Gives me a very clear perspective.
Of what this life is.

For one thing, I am sure:
It's full of tests and tribulations
For a believer like me.
I have to think rationally
Rather than emotionally.
I have to move on,
Not be stuck up here on my own.
So be strong, I hear a whisper.
Take the path below.
For surely, as long one has life
One has to strive.
I know my Rabb will help.
He is there for me and has always been.
All I need is to trust Him.
He will surely heal me.
Life is sometimes not what you plan,
What you aim for.
Indeed, it is always how Allah intends.
And He is the Best of Planners
Though my heart shattered
Endless tears
My aching soul
Is all to purify me?
I convince myself
That my Lord's way
Is the only way for me?
So VERY SOON I will look
Into all my blessings
Promise to help others
Just like Allah has done Miracles
For me and my family

My parents named me Atiya
(A gift)
Which I hope I am for others
I am very, very tired and tearful
But full of Hope for the coming years

I shared this poem with my writing coach, Henrietta Szovati, during one of our sessions. She gently encouraged me to take the path below and not remain stranded on the cliff—assuring me with quiet optimism that I would be fine.

Whirling Confusion

Qayum began losing his balance, and I would often find him on the floor, particularly in the shower and TV lounge. I understood that people with dementia were at higher risk of falling due to issues with mobility, balance and muscle weakness, among other factors. It was a misconception that people with dementia only saw signs of neurological decay, as it was, in fact, a decay of the physicality and everything anatomically in the body. While medication can sometimes be a culprit, Qayum was not dependent on any medication from 2018 to 2019. I attended several courses on dementia, and I learned that patients were prone to hip fractures, which led to further complications such as pressure sores, infections and increased mortality, to name a few. This knowledge only increased my anxiety as I knew these were inevitable symptoms that were going to have a severely detrimental impact on my life, as well as the rest of my family. To mitigate the risks, I removed any potential hazards, such as rugs, from areas accessible to Qayum, as well as risky furniture like coffee tables and stools. I removed any bathroom locks in case he accidentally locked himself inside, and I always accompanied him on the staircase. Qayum struggled to navigate the vertigo that came with walking up or down the steps. I also installed sturdy handrails on the staircase and in the bathrooms, courtesy of Mediquip. Additionally, his bedroom was relocated downstairs for easy access to the washroom. The design of the house was set up in such a way as to ensure the home was as practical, safe and comfortable as possible for my role as a permanent carer and for my dear Qayum. I had labelled everything for Qayum, including the door, kettle, and taps, so he could easily locate them, but by then, Qayum had lost all his comprehension skills.

Falls were frequent, and each time, I was nervous and expecting the worst. I would call 111, and they would come and check him thoroughly and make some light-hearted jokes to lighten the mood. They would place him on his favourite settee, and all would be good—at least temporarily. Qayum had the gift of forgetfulness, which would leave him mindlessly repeating the same act that would lead him to fall again. The constant vigilance was exhausting, but I didn't want him to suffer a fracture. But by now, Qayum had very little capacity left to express himself, causing an even greater void and drift between us. All Qayum could do was respond to some of my *salaams*, although it was a somewhat distorted greeting. Most of the time, I followed Qayum's lead, but many other times, I was the giver through Allah's mercy. Allah's names, Al-Rahman and Al-Raheem, were names I chose to internalise and manifest those characteristics. Both the attributes of Allah demonstrate His extreme mercy. The difference between the two is that Rahman indicates the extensive nature of His mercy; hence, it is translated as "All Merciful", while Raheem refers to its intensive quality and, therefore, it is rendered as Very Merciful. If Allah was able to show us compassion despite our constant shortcomings, pitfalls and sinning, then how could I hold back my compassion for Qayum?

Each day, I grew in my connection with Qayum. Hardship gave me a new lens to see through by amplifying my compassion and empathy for him. I realised I was extremely patient and tolerant on some days; on some, I was trying to just get by, and on others, I didn't even want to be near Qayum. Just getting to bed each day in one piece, with every single part of my body aching, felt like the greatest victory. On those bad days, I sought Allah's help and guidance as I felt a gaping void without Him by my side, and I needed all the patience I could muster just to get by. Despite the difficulties, Qayum's illness taught me the meaning of possessing unwavering strength, respect, patience, compassion, love and sacrifice. His dementia was a profound gift, teaching me to be mindful and present with him and appreciate the beauty of slowing down and relishing in those precious, finite moments. I learned the art of connection, the true meaning of love being synonymous with service, and how to quickly adapt to his needs, however difficult or unreasonable they may be. I learned that happiness is not found in external things but within myself. If I wanted happiness, I was going to create it. If I wanted compassion, I needed to give it to others. And if I sought Allah's mercy, I needed to embody it and show it first of all to my husband and then to others who need it.

Of course, there were times of impatience and frustration, feeling like a complete failure. Those moments made me feel so helpless and alone. It was difficult to accept that the connection was going to remain one-sided and unreciprocated, as he was no longer just my husband but my Alzheimer's patient. The disease was eroding his sense of being, and day by day, I felt I was losing more of Qayum. It was an erosion of the self, happening in slow motion, prolonging the pain and suffering I was experiencing. Yet, I was determined to stay connected to Qayum through the fragments of his soul and his tangled mess of words.

In those moments, I could see Qayum's teary eyes as if he were trying to thank me. In his disoriented speech, I could catch glimmering glances of the love and compassion he had reserved for me—a love built on labour, sweat, and tears, a love that eventually saw the light over those forty-plus years.

Those moments of pure connection and love were all I needed to keep going, reassuring me that I was doing okay. It was like a gentle whisper telling me: "You're doing well, my darling. I am proud of you."

"If only you knew how much I love you."

"Oh, Atiya, how debilitated I feel at this moment; I am so sorry."

"You have no idea how alone I feel right now."

"I hate being this reliant on you...."

"I am sorry, my darling. This is not what I envisaged for our life together the moment I said, 'I do.'"

I was also reminded of Arne Garorg's words:

> *"To love a person is to learn the song that is in their heart and to sing it to them when they have forgotten."*

And so, I found myself learning every hymn and chorus of Qayum's soul, singing them repeatedly through the shadows of our struggles.

Chapter Eleven

Living with Alzheimer's

Returning to Learning

In 2018, I was invited by my GP at Elliott Hall Medical Centre to take part in a research study at UCL, aimed at helping carers of Alzheimer's patients navigate the uncharted territory of the disease with greater care and sensitivity. The study was led by Dr. Nathan Davies, Senior Research Fellow. I was eager to help Qayum, I seized the opportunity. I was also keen to join other like-minded people who were in the same boat as me, struggling with their mental health and wanted to be equipped with the knowledge, care and support required. I wanted to feel I had an enriching and educated community I could turn to at any time. Listening to the group, I felt tears in my eyes, trying to fathom the grim years ahead of Qayum and the extent of pain and suffering he was about to endure. It disturbed me, but I reminded myself that it was God's plan for my family, and I needed to have faith.

Dr. Pushpa Nair, a team member at UCL, invited me to a

study session on "Eating, drinking, and care for people with dementia at the end of life: How can we best support family carers?" At first, I was taken aback by the idea of Qayum being at the end of his life, and I petitioned never to join. I knew Qayum still had a long way to go before I could classify him as coming to an end, and I wasn't ready to delve into the later stages of his suffering. However, the research was greatly beneficial, and I managed to contribute through my reading.

In June 2020, I joined another research study titled "An exploration of the impact of Covid-19 on dementia care in Black and Minority Ethnic Groups." The study couldn't have come at a better time, with the pandemic creating ambiguity, confusion and fear amongst the Alzheimer's community—a community already struggling as it is and heavily dependent on human networking and face-to-face interactions.

Furthermore, I participated in a PhD proposal study examining person-centred care, care environments, and care planning for individuals with dementia from South Asian backgrounds in the UK. It was a three-year study that began in January 2023, focusing on the importance of understanding the care environment and the cultural factors that influence person-centred care.

This matter was crucial and pressing for not only those who were suffering from dementia, a disease fraught with uncertainty and unpredictability—but also the carers, who were arguably struggling more with the increasing demands for care while navigating the loss of their loved one. The issue also highlighted the importance of understanding the care environment and the cultural factors that influence person-centred care. Of course, I was biased as it was my own community in question, but regardless of race or colour, I wanted to immerse myself in all the studies and literature concerning this topic and truly make a difference.

With my first-hand contributions to the research, all that was left was to await the outcomes. Fortunately, Dr. Nair valued my input and believed it would help the South Asian communities.

Reminisce

One evening, before Qayum had lost his ability to speak coherently, he begged me to take him to Pakistan to visit his deceased mother, who had passed away in 1998 and his siblings. He wanted to ask his mother for a wife and discuss it with his siblings. I could see that Qayum was slipping into the past. When I told him he was already married, he was shocked and asked, "To whom?" I made sure I chose my words wisely, reassuring him it was to someone he deeply loved. I also promised to look into flights for our trip to Pakistan, knowing that with his memory issues, he wouldn't even remember the conversation. However, I couldn't help but reflect on how his past had morphed into his present. It was as if Qayum's resistance and refusal to let go of those parts of him were his way of honouring our treasured bond. SubhanAllah.

I retrieved our wedding album to share and retell old family stories, trying to address his feelings without causing him pain. It was heartbreaking to see Qayum nodding at each picture, overwhelmed by emotions and unable to make sense of his world.

Walking on Edges

By 2019, after five challenging years, life at home became increasingly difficult. One day, Qayum shocked me with an earnest apology, confessing he was sorry for giving me such a difficult time. I was stunned to speak at that moment, for I felt, almost momentarily, that my unvoiced feelings were validated and understood; I needed to savour that moment, for I knew it was unlikely for it to come by again. However, I gently assured him that it was not his fault and that we would get through this rough patch together.

"Can you tell me what's happening to me?" he asked in a solemn tone.

With a sinking heart and a cracked voice, I replied, "You'll be fine, don't worry; you're just losing your memory, which is normal as we age."

When I first announced the news to Qayum, I explicitly told him he had Alzheimer's. He didn't respond, perhaps because, like me, he had never heard of it before and didn't fully understand what the disease entailed. As they say, ignorance is bliss. It was only once the blind ignorance morphed into inquisitiveness that I learned more about the disease, and with that knowledge, a surmountable fear and choking anxiety took hold.

Qayum began engaging in increasingly dangerous behaviour, leaving me in a constant state of vigilance and fear. One morning, I found him with a knife in his mouth, mistaking it for a toothpick. He was completely unaware of the risks around him, much like a child. I couldn't take my eyes off him for even a moment. To keep him safe, I had to "childproof" the entire house, hiding knives, scissors—anything that could cause harm.

On another occasion, I caught Qayum mixing honey with ketchup and eating it with a spoonful. The next morning, I discovered a mug filled with a pale yellow liquid, only to realise, to my horror, that it was his urine. It soon became clear that he had started urinating in different parts of the house and spitting in various corners of what was once our polished, beautiful home. The transformation was incomprehensible—this disease wasn't just consuming Qayum; it was unravelling both of our lives.

He found solace in simple, repetitive tasks—like carefully removing tissues from a box, folding them, and placing them back in neat order. Watching him offered me a brief moment of peace and a window into his quiet mindfulness and enduring curiosity. The difference between him and a child in that moment was stark: his actions were no longer a choice but a response to the impulses of his own mind, beyond his control.

A week later, when I showed him our wedding pictures again, he didn't recognise himself as the groom. He repeatedly asked, "That's you when you were young?" He made me feel like an alien and refused to accept the woman in the pictures as his wife. I wore a gold *passa* (a traditional hair ornament) and *mang tikka* (a forehead decoration), and although I understood it was the disease affecting him, it took me down memory lane. Alhamdulillah—Allah is the giver and taker of all gifts. Qayum had been a truly blessed and gifted person born on this earth.

Amidst all this turmoil, our family cat, Mau, whom I named and who was also known as Silver by my grandchildren, was deteriorating. At eighteen years old, his health was failing, and the vet recommended euthanasia. Juggling my allergies, Qayum's illness and Mau's decline was overwhelming. Qayum couldn't express his grief over our pet's loss. I vividly remember him searching by the door for Mau one evening. I told him Mau was unwell and at the vet, and that was the end of the story. I kept showing him pictures, but he could not respond. It was heartbreaking. I could sense that Qayum missed Mau deeply, especially since Mau had often sat on his lap or beside him. Mau, you were a cherished creation of my Lord, and I miss you dearly.

When Words Fall Apart

For over forty years, Qayum focused on making banking his priority. But once he became a victim of dementia, his mind still couldn't be taken off the bank. He was fixated on meeting the bank manager every single day. To ease his mind, I would gently divert his attention away by suggesting a walk, knowing within moments, he would forget about the bank entirely and just embrace forest bathing and soaking in the sun. Still, his thoughts were consumed by money—chequebooks, signatures—all garbled in his incoherent and fragmented speech. His harmless muses and wishful thinking turned into moments of confusion, rage and anger, as he alleged I was taking money from his wallet. To avoid any further accusations, I would leave a small amount of money in his wallet to show him every time he accused me. This small gesture seemed to soothe him, quenching the fire of his fury and keeping any arguments at bay. For Qayum, money represented power, independence and a sense of his own masculinity. From the moment he left home and embarked on his adventure overseas, money became his gateway to a better life. Even with dementia, he still seemed to cling onto that part of himself, as it gave him a sense of control and purpose. He was living in his perpetual, make-believe world of finance and banking, unable to relinquish the idea that I was now in charge of all our finances. Gradually, I noticed that Qayum's interest in his possessions was waning, which was a real shift from the man he once was, who was always well-groomed, chic and meticulously cared for.

Early in his illness, we had the foresight to establish Power of Attorney (POA) for both of us, including our children, when it came to any matters relating to health and finances. This meant that Qayum was able to hand over any of his legal, financial and medical matters to us so we could manage our affairs responsibly and fairly. Such an intervention proved to be the best decision we made—a saving grace and blessing for the darker days ahead when Qayum lost his capacity entirely.

Bathing and dressing are such individual and deeply personal tasks that one would never expect that a day would come when it would be this early on that a transfer of duty would be necessary. As Qayum's illness progressed, these tasks became increasingly difficult. I would prepare everything for the shower, giving him a pre-warning that in five minutes, I would be bathing him. In hindsight, I should have accounted for more time, as Qayum's reluctance and resistance often meant we were going back and forth for over twenty minutes discussing why he needed to shower. I would assure him the water was warm to his liking and his best clothes were ready. He hated the idea of being taken out of his comfort zone and being put under the shower on a stool, where he'd get wet and sticky. I resorted to a helpful tactic: playfully waving my hand in front of my nose, suggesting that he was starting to smell. Somehow, that worked. Qayum seemed to retain some dignity and consideration for me, not wanting to see himself in a situation involving unpleasant body odour. Once in the shower, Qayum would cooperate. Although the process was exhausting, I felt a sense of accomplishment. I knew it was more than a bath; it was an opportunity to get him looking as clean and sharp as ever. Each day, his resistance lessened, and I reminded myself to stay calm and collected.

As the disease advanced, I had to give his wardrobe a makeover, appropriate for a husband who was becoming increasingly unwell. I bought him pants with elastic waistbands, loose-fitting tops, easy-to-wear socks, and slip-on shoes with Velcro closures.

Despite everything, I made sure Qayum was always dressed smartly from the moment he woke up. I wanted to honour a tradition he held dear—dressing for the day before enjoying his morning tea. In my many years of marriage, I never saw Qayum lounging in a robe or dressing gown; dressing him down in such attire would have done a disservice to his dignity and pride.

Our regular visits to the dentist became my acts of kindness. I wanted to maintain a sense of normalcy and routine for Qayum with his routine check-ups, appointments and medical visits. I am forever grateful to Mr. Hutchinson and his team at Rayners Lane Dental Surgery for their consistent kindness towards Qayum and for being gentle and considerate even when he could no longer communicate. While it is understandable that one might become impatient and inconsiderate in such situations, this was not the case for Mr. Hutchinson.

When it came to meals, Qayum's appetite was still the same, although his palate had changed. I needed to adjust my cooking to cater to his tastes by reducing the amount of spices and preparing fresh meals daily. He was not one to complain and scoffed down anything I made him, but after twenty years of eating oats, he suddenly couldn't stomach the texture or taste of it, so I removed it from the breakfast menu.

Our visits to the Bridge Centre became our treasured outings. While Abdul Qayum didn't join the exercises since he was unable to follow the instructions, sitting and occasionally uttering a word seemed to bring him some comfort. For me, the talking therapy sessions were invaluable, offering a space to share my struggles with others who were in similar situations. It was during these moments that I realised true empathy comes from those who have felt the sting of shared suffering.

In the Shadow of the Pandemic

In December 2019, the world was shaken by the news of a mysterious virus emerging from Wuhan, China. By March, Covid-19 had been declared a pandemic by the World Health Organisation, and for us, it was a double blow.

Qayum watched the news, although he couldn't comprehend what was happening. I could see the confusion, fear and panic in his eyes while he was unable to express his concerns. As things got increasingly unwary, I tried to protect him from the outside world. And then, suddenly, it was January 2020—cold, freezing, and isolating. I understood how seasonal depression could truly take hold, compounding a feeling of cabin fever, lower mood, and diminished serotonin levels. The darkness settled in the sky early in the day, casting a gloomy and foreboding atmosphere.

Looking back, I can say that the COVID-19 pandemic was a cruel and unforgiving time for everyone. I had taken for granted the little pockets of joy that Bridge Centre had brought me through my weekly exercises. The simple pleasures of life, like hand-selecting the ripest tomatoes and apples, felt like distant memories. The support I was receiving was terminated; carers no longer stopped by, doctors only communicated by phone, and I had to rely on online shopping for groceries.

Despite all this, I was grateful for the walks I was able to take Qayum on twice a day, as well as the drives through the countryside. It became increasingly difficult to get Qayum in the car, so I bought a handle-like gadget to assist him, although it remained a struggle.

During a brisk afternoon, we drove to Pinner Memorial Park for a change of scenery. As we sat beside each other quietly by the lake, watching the birds soar, flutter and cruise the skies before our eyes, Qayum burst out ecstatically: "Aeroplane!" I was taken aback at that moment, processing how an Alzheimer's-ravaged mind was still able to make a connection between the birds and an aeroplane. It was a moment to cherish—a fleeting glimpse of my husband's enduring spark of intelligence, a remnant of the man he once was.

On our car journeys, I would keep Qayum engaged by giving him a running commentary on the weather, the people on the street, and the colours around us, including the trees and plants we were surrounded by. It was as though I had my young child in the backseat of the car, curious like a sponge, ready to take in whatever new knowledge or information I was about to share. A child who was relying on me to share a glimpse of the world and how to look at it. As we approached one familiar street, I pointed at a tree that looked particularly abysmal and dreary. To my surprise, Qayum responded, with a touch of unintended wit, that the tree needed a shower. We both laughed heartily and for a moment, it felt like complete bliss. A momentary stillness infused with joy, humour and warmth away from the cold February afternoon and the chill of my all-consuming worries and anxieties. Those moments were truly treasured blessings from Allah, offering a reprieve from the virus-laden, anxiety-compounded spaces that consumed us all.

The pandemic inflicted turmoil, especially for young children and the elderly, never mind those with dementia. By then, Qayum had lost 85% of his cognitive capacity, rendering the epidemic an abstract notion for him. I knew burdening him with the details of the pandemic would be not only unnecessary but also counterproductive. His frequent dizziness and loss of balance were direct symptoms of his urinary infections. Further, moments of lightheadedness caused his falls and injuries, leading to numerous visits from the paramedics.

To ensure Qayum's safety, I installed a baby monitor to keep a vigilant eye on him while he was settled downstairs. I couldn't risk any more injuries as a result of him attempting to navigate the flight of stairs. The thought of him struggling with those treacherous steps that once seemed so benign—filled me with dread. The monitor became more than a tool but a lifeline, offering me peace of mind away from the relentless fear that Qayum was in danger.

In times of such profound hardship, I found solace in my faith. I took comfort in knowing that Allah, in his infinite wisdom, was going to look after me. As Al-Alim (The All-Knowing), He is aware of everything that has happened and will happen in the future. Destiny is already written, and for that reason, there is nothing left but to be present at the moment and live consciously according to Allah's guidelines. Acts of kindness, sincerity of action, and the art of letting go—while trusting in Allah's wisdom—became necessary ingredients for a life that is both enriching and more divinely attuned.

The absence of support from carers became extremely overwhelming. The 24-hour days felt like they stretched into 36-hour ones. I found myself plagued by thoughts of what might happen if I fell ill, became completely incapacitated, or, God forbid, passed away. My mind raced through countless worse-case scenarios, consumed by worry about Qayum and the kids. The only connection with the outside world was through phone calls. However, since Qayum was losing his ability to communicate, those calls from friends gradually became futile. He showed no interest, and if he did speak, he would say: "Atiya has gone to work", abruptly ending the conversation and most probably discouraging them from calling again.

I began calling out to Allah devoutly for mercy and assistance, feeling choked by the restrictions imposed by COVID within my own home. I felt trapped and recalled the story of Yunus (AS) and the prayer he made in the belly of the whale. Knowing I had no one to turn to with my worries, I turned to reciting the dua of Yunus (AS):

> *La Ilaha Illa Anta Subhanaka Inni Kuntu*
> *Minaz Zalimin*
> *"There is no deity but you. Glory be to you.*
> *Truly, I have been of the wrongdoers."*
>
> ....
> **(Quran 21:87)**

In 2014, the late Shaykh Muhammad Alshareef (may his soul rest in peace) taught me, in one of his courses, the importance of praying with sincerity and seeking Allah's guidance earnestly. Now more than ever, I needed to make my dua as impactful, meaningful and as specific as possible. I prayed for good health, as I knew with good health, Qayum and l would be okay. Above all, I wanted to be present for Qayum in his final moments. I called out to Allah, confident He would answer, given there is goodness in it and the timing is right.

The situation reminded me of Hagar's story and her relentless *sa'i*—the pilgrim's journey between the hills of Safa and Marwa in search of relief. The complete trust she had in Allah, knowing that despite her exhaustion and desperation, Allah still looked after her and caused a spring of water, known as Zamzam, to gush forth in a desolate desert.

I knew I couldn't afford to be sick, not with the heavy weight of responsibility that lay on my shoulders. The mere thought of Qayum being taken away to a care home filled me with deep-seated guilt and dread. Each time I considered the possibility of it, it felt as though a knife had twisted in my heart. When I went to visit my GP, I withheld the full truth out of fear that I would be scrutinised or questioned. The doctor declared in an almost matter-of-fact, detached tone to consider a care home, with a sense of inevitability, as though it was the most sensible course of action. I nodded in agreement, displaying no sense of objection to her suggestion while inwardly rejecting every word.

The relentless cycle of overthinking left me sleepless, drained, and unable to fully process my emotions. As the final days of Ramadan approached, I knew I felt myself overcome by the crippling feeling of guilt for not being able to fast. I had fasted religiously since the age of twelve, never missing a day, but this year was different. My body, once resilient, felt frail and weak from the role of a caregiver. I knew the added strain of fasting would take a further toll on my body. I cried to Allah, upset for letting myself down. Ramadan ended, and Eid came along like a distant, unfamiliar guest. The government restrictions meant there were no Eid prayers or visitors, and the usual festive spirit was absent. Eid, which was once a much-awaited joyous occasion following the days of hunger, hardship and struggle, was now shadowed by a sense of isolation and sorrow.

The bare winter branches that we passed on our drives became symbols of peace and comfort to the weary hearts and afflicted spirits, a reminder of the unyielding beauty and solace amidst our trials.

When Eid Took a Turn

The dawn of Eid day began with a sense of joy and anticipation. I woke early, eager to embrace the festivity. As I went downstairs, I found Qayum still sleeping peacefully. I seized the opportunity to shower and put on my outfit that was laid out meticulously on my bedside the night before, ready to begin my day with a clean spirit and body. This was not just a routine but a cherished *sunnah* practice, essential on Eid day, connecting me to every Muslim around the world who was also celebrating Eid. Grateful for another day, I went back downstairs; however, to my surprise, Qayum was on the floor in an alarmingly strange position, and he did not look okay. To this day, I still struggle to understand what had happened to Qayum.

By this stage, Qayum's communication had deteriorated significantly. He could only manage a few fragmented words that, most times, made no sense. Knowing that we couldn't converse left me with no option but to call emergency services. The paramedics arrived promptly, but Qayum was disoriented and not cooperating. His only response was a resolute "NO!" as he was asked to be assessed.

The NHS paramedics were extremely patient and waited until Qayum was ready to be treated. After forty-five minutes of effort and consoling him, they managed to get him a wheelchair and comfort him as best as they could. Given the restrictions imposed by COVID-19, I was prepared for the worst and knew I couldn't accompany Qayum to Northwick Park Hospital, leaving me utterly heartbroken and tearful. I knew how much this would mean to Qayum, but also for myself, for my own sanity. Waiting for an update from the hospital, knowing I could do nothing to help, was the most distressing ordeal.

Three hours later, I called the hospital for an update. They informed me they had just completed an x-ray and CT scan and were waiting for the results. Another three hours had passed before I learned that Qayum had suffered a hip fracture and required immediate surgery. My heart ached, knowing I couldn't be with him at such a crucial moment of his life. I wept myself to sleep, the weight of guilt eating away at me. Our Eid day was plagued by the memory of his departure from home. I felt an ominous sense that this might be Qayum's departure from our home forever, and tragically, I was right. It was an inevitable and sorrowful day that I tried to shut down in my mind, but which I equally knew was coming. Qayum never returned home after his fall.

No one prepares you for the profound emptiness you feel once your role as a caregiver is revoked and you resume back to normal duties. It's a bittersweet truth, realising that this title—once filled with such demand, yet purpose was your antidote, your peace and the threads that held you together. Now, with this chapter closed, you mourn the parts of yourself that, though they once seemed to be pain and duty, were actually a vital thread of connection between us.

As the thread of caregiving is gently pulled away, you find yourself taking on the role of a seamstress tasked with stitching the pieces of your life back together. Each stitch is delicate, every weave purposeful, representing a core memory and a part of you that you cannot ignore. The hands that once mended others are now empty and chillingly staring back at me, waiting to mend themselves and craft a new sense of self from the threads of memory, grief, and loss.

Breaking Ground

In July 2024, I learned about new research carried out by Jo Brown from King's College London exploring the right to a care supporter. The research provided a glimmer of hope for dementia patients and the support that could be offered to them in the long run. Despite COVID-19 no longer posing an imminent global health crisis, there are still many local outbreaks of illnesses that impose temporary restrictions. Care home managers face the challenge of balancing potential infection outbreaks and the need for patients to be in contact with their families.

Research has shown the importance of social connection for health and how limiting such a basic human need could have cataclysmic and often irreversible effects. For some, the presence of a friend or family member is not only desirable but incumbent—whether it is the heartfelt and encouraging words from a spouse or the tender touch of a parent or child. Unpaid carers provide practical and emotional support that mimics professional care. As a result, John's campaign pledged to support unpaid carers in over 1,500 hospitals and care homes.

Furthermore, the Gloria's Law campaign, led by Care Rights UK and John's Campaign, advocates the right for a care supporter to be codified in UK law. This led to the Care Supporter Bill, ensuring that anyone receiving health or social care access to unrestricted in-person support from an essential care supporter. This was no one-off bill but a fully-fledged law that was monitored and enforced by regulators.

Under the pandemic restrictions, I was unable to visit Qayum in the hospital. Our only contact was via phone calls to the ward, where doctors and nurses provided updates. Each call was a reminder of how dire the situation was and how helpless I was feeling. Each day was a reminder of our helplessness and lack of power and Allah's infinite capabilities.

I wasn't ready to lose Qayum so soon. The slow, unrelenting progression of Alzheimer's had already made us lose him years before his literal departure. In those profoundly unsettling and dark moments, I turned to Allah, deeply grasping the meaning of *Inna lillahi wa inna ilayhi raji'un*, Indeed, to Allah we belong, and to Him we shall return. Knowing that ultimately, we do not belong to this world, nor to ourselves, but to Allah. It brought a profound shift in perspective, illuminating how little power or control we have over our lives.

Two days later, Dr. M called to let me know that Qayum was refusing to eat and was giving him a really hard time. The staff were now calling him Abdul, his first name, and he responded well to this sudden change in his name. The news was overwhelming, but I seized the opportunity to visit him despite knowing how difficult it was going to be to see him in such a dire state. I was given strict instructions to ensure his safety, as well as mine, including avoiding touching lift buttons, wearing disposable gloves and, of course, fresh PPE.

Visiting was restricted, and it only made matters more difficult for it felt pressured, time conditioned and sparse. Over the next six weeks, I was not prepared for the heart-wrenching reality of Qayum's condition as his delirium worsened. He became restless and confused, requiring medication to calm his nerves and being fitted with restraint gloves to stop him from removing essential lines and tubes. However, this was only causing him more distress and anger.

I knew Qayum was only going to deteriorate under these conditions, particularly given the stress that was hard to manage.

In the ward, Qayum was unable to communicate, but that did not stop people from showing their care and concern for him. As Qayum awaited his results, doctors and nurses were supportive as they asked for regular updates and their own forms of devotion and prayers—whether that was to Jesus or calls to Ram. I, too, called to Allah, humbled by the multiple prayers that were directed at Qayum. I prayed that Allah would accept their pleas and keep their spirits shielded and protected under

His wings of mercy. Even in the darkest of days, I was humbled to witness these guardian angels that Allah sent out our way to look after Qayum.

Surah Al-Fatiha is a reminder of the sense of unity and collectiveness of faith. It is also a reminder of Allah's compassion and mercy that are boundless and infinite. He listens to all and guides us when we need such guidance and mercy.

A few weeks later, I was heartbroken to learn that Qayum was never to walk again. This was after his condition had deteriorated in the hospital, an inevitable outcome given his condition. It's often said that ten days of rest equates to ten years of muscle ageing. This was indeed the case for Qayum, as his functionality declined. The lack of exercise due to COVID restrictions further hindered his rehabilitation journey. My attempts to assist with physiotherapy were in vain, as Qayum struggled to follow instructions. However, the nursing staff and doctors continued to be incredibly kind and supportive, providing us both with comfort and care. One doctor, though fully aware of Qayum's grim prognosis, reassured me with the faith that life and death are not in the doctor's hands but Allah's. He also referenced some miracles he witnessed in his time as a doctor.

I am beyond grateful for their genuine care, unwavering support, and the light and hope they brought into my life—it was evident that, to them, this was more than just a job.

Part IV
Closure and Reflection

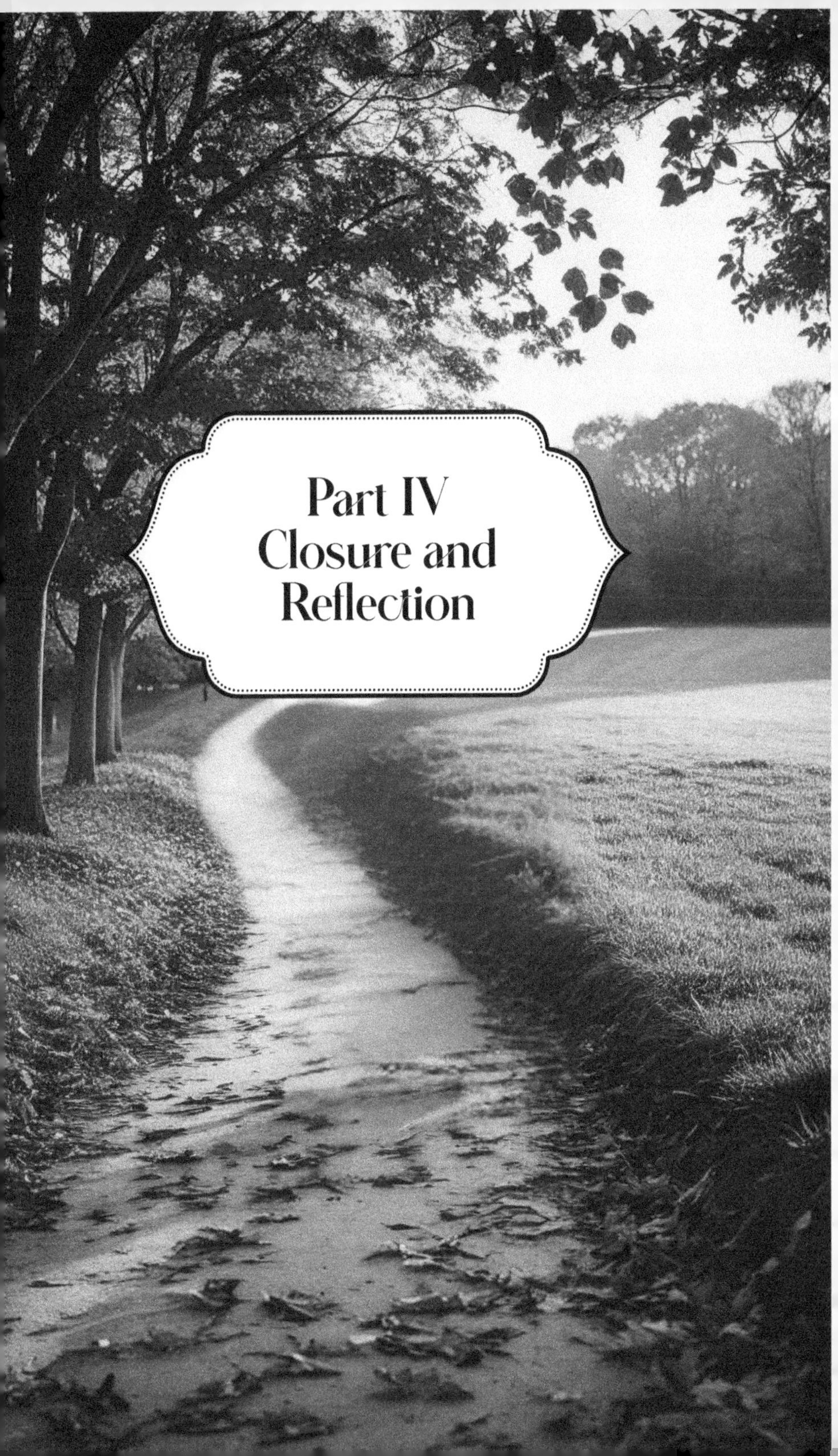

CHAPTER TWELVE

———✦———

DECLINE, LEGACY, CLOSURE, AND ACCEPTANCE

The Turning Tide

There was a heaviness in my heart, a sense of misery, knowing of the disastrous journey that lay ahead. I was already so exhausted, and I couldn't imagine things getting any worse. It was one trial followed by another, like a cascade of misfortunes—a car breaking down, a fridge malfunctioning, or a roof leaking. Oftentimes, it felt like I was being engulfed by it all, aimlessly wandering, lost and bewildered in the dense fog. The doctors offered no help or clear answers. Yet, trusting in Him was essential for healing. It involved believing that Allah's love for me was sufficient and accepting whatever trials and tribulations came with it.

On Friday, July 10th, at 1:30 pm, a ward nurse called to say they were transferring Qayum to a nursing home. This was the dreaded day I had hoped wouldn't ever come. I immediately protested and informed her that there was no way I would concede to this decision. Unfortunately, my words fell on deaf ears, and the nurse replied dismissively, offering me the choice of five homes to pick from. My heart sank, realising that no amount of protest was going to change fate or where Qayum would be residing that night and for his remaining days.

Five minutes later, the discharge nurse called, insisting he had to leave that afternoon. Once again, I refused, fully aware that my response would be met with indifference—if not outright dismissal. She followed up by saying that visits would not be allowed for some time due to COVID restrictions. My heart sank again, and I felt a surge of panic and anger take over me. I could no longer think or see straight. The thought of Qayum, who was already so ill, being transported like a sack of potatoes without my consent to a completely unfamiliar place with potential caregivers and social workers who might not provide him with the care he needed left me arrested by an overwhelming sense of dread, an icy state of panic and bone-deep fear.

Given the added restrictions due to COVID-19, I understood all the red tape and struggles I was about to face, but I could not grasp the insensitivity of some people who showed little care or support for Qayum. Following my refusal to leave Qayum in an unknown care home, they eventually reached a compromise, agreeing that he would remain under the care of the hospital staff; however, I felt like an outsider—unwelcomed and ignored.

One afternoon, a nurse told me with a tinge of resentment, "Qayum has been far too spoiled here; it's time he goes elsewhere." I was taken aback by her words, and she left the ward, perhaps realising how her words were uncalled for and cruel. It underscores the widespread lack of understanding about Alzheimer's—a complex disease with countless challenges and complications. With the mind being so complex and unique, so too was the disease, with its myriad of symptoms and sinister, Qayum's irritability and forgetfulness, but also in more significant losses that took away his individuality and authenticity. I had expected more compassion and a deeper understanding from trained professionals, considering their responsibility to be trauma-informed and empathetic, but it was sadly wishful thinking.

When I went to see Qayum, I couldn't believe how ghastly and expressionless he looked. I wondered what was going on in his mind—or perhaps there was nothing. All his belongings were packed up and left near him, marking the beginning of his displacement. No one seemed to consider how vulnerable Qayum was at that moment. All I wanted to do was cuddle him and stand by him. Fortunately, I could speak English fluently; I knew the NHS and understood the complexity of his disease far better than all those working on the ward that day. I had lived with this illness for six gruelling years until it became part of me. Every year, month, day, minute and second came with the loss of Qayum and the death of another of his cells. It was heart-wrenching witnessing the extent of suffering he was about to endure.

When I entered the ward at 5 o'clock, I found Qayum looking so confused and agitated, his mouth full of vomit and chocolate, his gown shabby and stained. I felt utter rage and called for the nurse to check on Qayum. He was left unattended from noon to 5pm, and I was in complete disbelief. It felt deliberate, as though they were punishing me or him.

Besides their general negligence, it was clear they were also lacking in basic clinical care. They failed to check his blood pressure and perform other necessary medical checks. Qayum clearly looked unwell. He was showing slight improvement but remained unable to communicate. I left at 7pm, my heart heavy with helplessness and despair, the image of Qayum's pale complexion lingering in my mind. His eyes were empty of all expression, almost like they were void of any emotion or hope.

All I could wonder was, how had we ended up in this situation? Me, his once dedicated sole carer, away from my beloved, frail husband. He was now under the care of so-called professionals who were not doing their job properly.

As I was about to leave, a nurse told me Qayum would be transferred on Monday, July 13th. I didn't know whether to feel relieved or saddened by the news, knowing how bad Qayum's current experience was. Was the change going to be good for him and finally bring him the care he needed, or was it only going to compound his confusion? There were far too many unpredictable variables to even process what was happening, so I decided to leave a note at the desk listing precisely what my demands were for Qayum. I demanded a dementia-registered nursing home for Qayum, an opportunity to discuss his needs via consultations, my consent and approval for any decisions, and a thorough financial assessment. I was not only speaking on behalf of Qayum but also of any victim battling a deadly disease. They deserved the clinical and human care that a loved one would offer at home.

I was a strong, educated Muslim woman who was taught to speak up and fight for what was right. My upbringing instilled in me a fierce determination to fight against oppression and use my voice to make change. I could not be a bystander and watch Qayum deteriorate by the day. I knew I would continue to fight for my husband until his final breath. With every bold-spoken gesture and act of service that Qayum dedicated to us in our marriage, I was now his voice and advocate in these silent moments of suffering and pain.

A Rock in the Storm

I needed to garner the strength to write an official complaint about what had happened to Qayum on Friday, which I intended to deliver to the doctors on duty. The PALS (Patients Advisory Liaison Service) office was closed due to the pandemic, which was not the worst part—but being ignored by the ward staff was. Fortunately, there was a senior consultant who was gracious enough to read the letter and offer me comfort.

I hadn't known the extent of the struggles that Qayum had faced, such as being turned down by several nursing homes, until I received a formal response from PALS in September 2020. The response stated that my husband was medically fit, and they went on to cover their faults, making me feel like an absolute fool seeking drama and attention.

At times, I couldn't help but wonder if I was taken less seriously as a visible hijabi woman of South Asian descent. Despite being a loyal citizen who has called this country home for over 50 years and always contributing to society, I sometimes felt a lingering sense of not fully belonging. Worse yet, I feared that no matter how much I tried, true acceptance would always be just out of reach.

A meeting was arranged with a senior nurse and a different staff member who was responsible for nursing home transfers. I was offered tissues and some water as a conciliatory gesture, for I was about to be told some bad news. I really wanted the nursing home manager to be present, but she was unavailable. I was told I was not fit to care for my husband at home and that there was no option but for him to move to a nursing home right away.

On Monday, July 13th, 2020, Abdul Qayum was transferred to a nursing home. Due to the pandemic, I was unable to visit or see how the place looked inside, but eventually, I was permitted some socially distanced visits. The staff assured me he was being offered halal food, kept clean and given excellent care in general. In my lowest points, when I was all alone, I clung to these words for hope. Leaving him there for the first time, I screamed and cried in agony all the way home, hoping with every shriek, Allah was hearing me and offering me relief, and with every silent cry, the staff would take it as a plea to truly care for Qayum. The guilt was crushing and all-consuming.

I desperately hoped the manager was true to her words and cared for Abdul Qayum in the way I was promised.

The Sinking Ship

The emptiness and void I felt when Qayum was away felt like a gaping hole that was slowly eating away at me. My children, far away, had to be strong for me while I kept feeling guilt, shame and a sense of remorse.

Talking to other carers was the only time I felt understood, realising it was a feeling that never ever fades. It's like grief or any other similar intense emotion tied to a deep love you have for someone, followed by a loss. The guilt came from not having the privilege to care for Qayum at home until the end, to be with him as his illness continued to gnaw away at him and as he eventually departed this world.

I had to admit defeat in the face of these carers who had taken my place. Qayum no longer recognised me, his eyes vacant, and that unfamiliar gaze compounded my pain. It's like the knot that bound us together was severed right before my eyes. There was no longer "Qayum and I". There was only Atiya—the grieving widow-to-be, watching from afar, and her husband, lost in the fog of Alzheimer's, who was perishing. Watching him slip away while still physically present was a painfully paradoxical and unexplainable feeling.

In the days when the thought of death alone was in the back of my mind, I was reminded of the name of Allah, Al-Muhyi, the Giver of Life. Everything lives because Allah willed it to, and everything perishes when Allah wills it to. We are nothing but travellers in this world, and with each passing day, a part of us goes. I prayed to Allah, calling out his name, Al-Muhyi, to do what is best for me and Qayum. I knew this was a test, and it would pass. I knew that Qayum and I would be okay and that Allah would reunite us in a place of eternal happiness, free from sickness, in Jannah. There was nothing that was going to change destiny, but I had power over my thoughts and perspective. I had power over my faith, and those were the things I busied myself with. The closer I came to Allah, the closer I felt Him to me.

The Prophet Muhammad (ﷺ) said:

> *"Allah the Almighty said: 'I am as My servant thinks of Me, and I am with him as he remembers Me. If he draws near to Me with a hand span, I draw near to him an arm's length. And if he draws near to Me an arm's length, I draw near to him a fathom's length. And if he comes to Me walking, I go to him running.'"*

(Sahih al-Bukhari 7405, Sahih Muslim 2675)

Every day, I faced a choice: whether to recluse and stay away from Allah and remain isolated in my own sorrows or to draw nearer to Him even by an inch to find true peace and comfort. The effort we put in turning towards Allah is never in vain.

I knew the more distance I experienced, the more I allowed

myself to be prey to the Shaytan—his devilish whispers and insidious influence thrived in my weak, fragile, and consumed state, sabotaging my thoughts and mental state.

Shaytan's darkness is not just an abstract concept of evil and mere whispering; it is a consuming abyss that feeds on our fears, doubts and insecurities, leaving us to spiral into a deeper state of worthlessness and hopelessness. The whispers are like poison to the soul, compounding our isolation, grief and helplessness. Yet, in the midst of this darkness, the only light we find within us is the Divine light that faith and closeness to Allah brings, dispelling even the deepest shadows.

Living Under Storm Clouds

I was given the name of the nursing home in Northwood, located on the border of Greater London and Hertfordshire. The upscale suburban area offered me some reassurance, yet I still drove with a heavy heart, tears flowing like a river. An overwhelming sense of uncertainty and fear weighed on me. The nursing home's website gave me some comfort, highlighting its ability to cater to a wide range of needs, including people with dementia. Knowing the staff were specialised gave me reassurance that these staff were specialised and equipped to handle Alzheimer's patients was crucial for my peace of mind.

The manager was graciously kind, assuring me that they served halal food and that most of the staff were Muslim men from an African background. They promised to provide good care of Qayum and recite his morning and evening supplications each day. Fortunately, I was living only ten minutes away, which meant I could technically visit anytime.

On the other side, I got unhelpful and judgmental remarks from well-meaning friends who were warning me against putting

Qayum in a care facility, assuming it was in my control. They did not understand my health condition or the predicament we were in, nor did I wish to waste my breath explaining to them. I was trying to conserve my energy for myself; I knew I needed it the most. Speaking up felt like a lost cause and, in some cases, even harmful. I was either yielding no benefit whatsoever from airing my concerns or witnessing many people who were taking pleasure in my misery. One friend told me to get in touch with a lady who may be able to care for Qayum; when I contacted her, she dryly and forthrightly told me she only cared for children, not grown men. There was a palpable atmosphere of judgement and silent scrutiny. How could I dispose of my husband, with such indifference, to an uncaring nurse who would treat him as an afterthought? I felt like I was closely monitored for my every move and decision, and with it came an evident air of judgement, disapproval and disappointment.

One person wrote to me and my family: "Your parents went out of their way to ensure you weren't placed in a care home when you were young, needy and dependent on them, and now you're betraying them, and putting them in a care home?"

Those words cut deeply as though a sharp dagger pierced and turned into my heart, with each syllable twisting and turning, leaving a lingering pain that was intent on staying. They were absolutely heartless to make such a comment. I responded by telling them not to message again and to wait for our verdict.

Ultimately, in the end, it was just me, Qayum and our children who were in this predicament. We knew there was no other option, and Allah was a witness to our vulnerability and powerlessness, and that's all that mattered.

When the news went out, I was extremely worried about the backlash I was going to receive, especially from Qayum's siblings.

However, Alhamdulillah, they were extremely supportive and understanding. I was so relieved to know they trusted me enough and recognised the undeniable and deep care I had for their brother, believing what I was doing was right and best for him, given the available options—or lack thereof.

Widespread Havoc

During the height of the COVID-19 pandemic, which took a toll on our lives, I visited Qayum every other day. I needed those alternate days to garner some strength and refuel. Qayum made the nurses' lives challenging by refusing every meal they tried to serve him, so I took on the task of preparing and delivering fresh, home-cooked meals every day. It was a labour of love and just one way I could show my love for Qayum and give him a feeling of a home away from home. I made sure to label each meal and date and deliver them in person. The sight of unwashed pots and pans in my kitchen served as a stark reminder of my dwindling energy, as these tasks seemed enormous and insurmountable.

Regardless of all the efforts I made, the burden of guilt was relentless. The support from family and friends was so comforting. Still, it didn't alleviate the emptiness and loneliness I experienced every night as I entered the house after being so immersed in Qayum's life for six years.

Despite my open-mindedness and cooperative attitude, gaining the trust of the carers at the nursing home proved difficult. The environment was overwhelming and emotionally taxing. The constant background noise—including unsettling language and interactions—felt inappropriate for Qayum's surroundings.

The nursing home, overwhelmed by the influx of patients and shortage of staff, meant that there was nothing conducive or tolerable in those spaces anymore.

The pandemic tore through care homes, causing widespread havoc. By February and March 2020, the virus had killed off many people, especially those with compromised immune systems and existing frailty. Residents in care homes suffered on an immense scale, as the set-up of these facilities and the close proximity of patients only worsened the spread.

The nursing home where Qayum was admitted had suffered countless losses. At that point, strict protocols were in place for visits, as per Public Health guidance, which advised against visiting care homes, barring exceptional circumstances. During this time, I could only see Qayum in the garden of his care home if I was lucky, but often, it was a quick procedural phone call from one of his carers giving me the lowdown on his condition and what he has been up to.

With time, matters only worsened as restrictions tightened and visits became impossible. I couldn't fathom the new reality that was imposed on us, knowing that all I could do now was look at Qayum through a glass door. His confusion was palpable as he muttered incoherent and unintelligible words, leaving anyone around him feeling confused. The sorts of games and activities the carers would organise included a guessing game, with Qayum spending days playing.

The carers' routines became a guessing game, with Qayum's days spent in the hall largely unresponsive. Despite having one-to-one support, his condition meant that activities and interactions were minimal, and his ability to follow instructions or engage in meaningful activities was severely limited.

Alzheimer's disease, a thief in the night, had stolen Qayum's precious memories, leaving him with only fragments of his former self. His once rich vocabulary was replaced by a struggle to communicate, with simple words and names slipping away.

As the disease progressed, Qayum's ability to speak and express himself diminished, leaving him reliant on non-verbal cues and emotional expressions.

In response, I sought new ways to connect with him. I provided the nursing home with colourful stampers, pens, paper, a memory box with family photos, and sensory toys. These items were chosen with Qayum's previous DIY skills in mind, with the hope of sparking some connection or recognition.

Despite my efforts, the progression of his illness was a constant reminder of the loss and despair. Every moment of his fading memory and every interaction that failed to engage him deepened the pain of his condition. Yet, in those moments of darkness, I continued to seek ways to bridge the gap between us, hoping to bring him some comfort and connection in his final days.

Soothing the Soul

One of the ways I tried to bring relief to Qayum was through a Fidget mitten, which was something common for all dementia patients. I knitted one for Qayum, adding buttons, zips and textured patches to keep his hands engaged. Qayum would sit quietly, clutching these small, familiar objects in his hands. I even brought him local newspapers, and though he'd flip through the pages, there was no spark of recognition or interest. He didn't want to hear me read anymore. To soothe him, I played the Quran from a cube, the verses acting as a steady comfort. Yet, what truly held his attention were the simplest things—he would endlessly fidget with the zippers on his cardigans or roll the edges of sheets, blankets, and tablecloths between his fingers. Hours would pass with him immersed in these small, repetitive movements. Beyond this, he asked for nothing. He didn't demand, didn't say a word. His curiosity was still there, but it was silent—he'd look around as if searching for something, but no words came to express it.

Experts say that those with dementia need activities that stimulate the right side of the brain and that they need engagement to keep them present. But Qayum defied this. No matter what I tried, his mind had already retreated into a quiet space of its own. By 2021, the March air was still cool as we sat in the nursing home, and I remember the day he tried to speak. He struggled with his words, and though his lips formed sounds, the only thing I could understand was, "I don't know what is happening," a rare moment of clarity in response to the chaos around us. It was noisy, and I had grown accustomed to redirecting him, offering gentle answers to his confusion.

Then, as if adding to his isolation, COVID cast its dark shadow over every aspect of our lives. Lockdowns came and went, each time more suffocating. The residential homes were hit hard, with strained services, loss of vital support, and visits reduced to watching him through a glass door. It was heartbreaking. The familiar faces were gone, replaced by workforce shortages and overwhelmed staff. When Qayum was transferred to the nursing home, his GP—the doctor who had known him for over 40 years—had changed. How could they do that? In a world where Qayum was already slipping away, they took away the one person who knew the nuances of his condition, temperament and medical struggles. It felt wrong, so deeply wrong. Continuity in care, especially in dementia, is everything, and yet it was taken from him just when he needed it most.

I still visited him regularly, pressed my hands against the cold glass separating us, trying to gauge his care, trying to trust them. Every time I raised a concern, I was met with the same polite response: "We'll look into it." And I trusted them. I had to. But doubt lingers when you cannot hold someone's hand and cannot see them fully cared for. It leaves you wondering—are they truly being looked after?

As Qayum's sole defender and spokesperson, the only person who truly had his back, I felt a heavy responsibility to represent him through his attorney while managing his healthcare and finances. I also sealed the Deprivation of Liberty Safeguards (DoLS) document, which clearly stated my duties—to maintain regular contact, represent and support Qayum in all matters, and provide supplementary care and assistance independent of the care home. I was his sole protector and lifeline, without whom he was unable to manage a day in the care home.

While I was confident in the care home's assistance and care, I already had some doubts they were going to give him the level of care I would expect for myself and any loved one. Yet, COVID-19 shattered even the most basic of systems, with GPs and physiotherapists no longer visiting, rather making their appointments virtual and no dietitian to look after Qayum's nutritional needs. While there was a nurse on site who was available around the clock, the reality was that nursing homes were congested and understaffed, which meant the quality of care patients received was massively compromised. There was no hope of witnessing exceptional care for the more complex conditions like Qayum's as their priority had shifted elsewhere to the more clinically sick.

From there on, I noticed Qayum's health was deteriorating rapidly, fuelled by cabin fever and separation from his loved ones. To make matters worse, I discovered that Qayum's one-to-one care, which I had been massively relying on, had been taken away. How was it that Qayum was going to be without undivided care and attention? The impact was immediate. Qayum, in his bottled-up anger, confusion and frustration, lashed out many times, throwing food and becoming deliberately difficult. The carers, who were already deeply frustrated and overworked, would complain to me, saying it wasn't fair that his care was terminated. Yet, the home manager showed no concern. It felt as though the nurses had taken all of Qayum's outbursts personally, frustratingly unable to separate his behaviour from his illness. Their ignorance about Alzheimer's was blatantly clear. Once again, I was feeling utter despair and hopelessness, and in that state, I found myself facing another test from Allah SWT. However, what was disheartening this time around was that I had such high hopes for this facility and its staff, and yet I felt so abandoned.

Through it all, I tried to remember that in this life, with all its trials and tribulations, was fleeting—just as my pain, my mental and emotional state was temporary, this too would pass, and I desperately clung to the hope of what Allah had in store for Qayum and I in Jannah.

I knew all this pain and struggle we had endured was not in vain

Divine Timing

One of Allah's names is Al-Hadi, the Guide. He never leaves us feeling stranded or abandoned; He lovingly directs us through the difficult terrains with clear signs if we turn to Him for guidance and direction. Al-Hadi had been guiding me all along, and in October 2021, the sign became so clear I knew I had to take action.

With Qayum's one-to-one carer being stripped away from him and the staff barely managing, I knew I had to take him out of there. The idea of a care home was already difficult enough; the thought of the compounded neglect was unfathomable. I needed Qayum to be in an environment that was Alzheimer's informed so the staff were professionally equipped to care for him in a manner that was befitting to his condition. So, I revisited a home I had considered for Qayum earlier. After speaking to the manager and waiting for my son Adnan to arrive from the USA, I finally found the inner peace that Qayum was finally going to be in an environment that would be full of tranquillity and greenery to match his love for nature.

I knew if he could speak, he would tell me this is where he wanted to spend his final days.

There were some comments circulating about whether it was appropriate to move someone so ill, as it may just add to their confusion and deterioration. But my certainty in Allah sufficed. I knew even if it had an immediate impact, Qayum would appreciate the transition and much prefer to be in a peaceful and professionally equipped place that prioritised his care. I continued to pray to Allah to look after Qayum and our family, knowing ultimately that Allah alone holds the answers to our struggles and tribulations.

Whenever I opened Allah's book, it was like Allah was directly speaking to me. I came across the verse as a reminder of His sovereignty and control over our lives:

"If Allah touches you with harm, none can undo it except Him. And if He touches you with a blessing, He is Most capable of everything."

(Surah Al-An'am, Verse 17)

The day finally arrived when we decided to move Qayum

from his Northwood nursing home. We arranged for a private ambulance to transfer Qayum comfortably to Buchanan Court Care Home. His new room was decorated to his taste, with pastel colours and surrounded by greenery; all we could see from his bed were trees swaying their bright green leaves and huge branches, which meant he was enveloped with peace and serenity. We made it to Qayum's final abode before his departure from this world. He looked around at the beautifully decorated room and gazed out at the trees and greenery; he immediately felt a sense of serenity and Zen. He muttered under his breath, "Very nice," and then added, "Bradford." Those were the words expressed by my beloved husband. Alhamdulillah, the next seven months of his life were spent in a place that offered him complete rest and rescue from the noise of others. He was blessed with carers who truly cared and communicated in a language he could understand. They did everything to keep him comfortable and happy. They fed him, took him to the lounge and did some routine strolls in a wheelchair as the disease continued to progress. They showed him respect and affection, especially with his dietary requirements and religious demands. They told me though Qayum cannot communicate, they love to look after him and give him their best. In them, I finally found comfort and peace knowing that Qayum was finally in the care of people who truly understood him and in a place that was the emblem of calm, peace, placid, serene and tranquillity. We as a family felt contented on this, which once again came as protection from Allah for someone who was so very ill and dying.

What do I say?
Where do I start
What do I say

My mind absolutely puzzled
At the passing away
I sit here and question my faith
Am I strong enough to face
Yes Allah, Yes Allah
You have been with me always
It's heart breaking and heavy
For my little tender loving soul
To be so much burdened that way
But my trust in my Lord
Keeps me strong everyday
The man I knew
Does not know me anyway
That is for sure, there is no cure
Friends and relatives
Ask for his well being
My reply now to them is
For all Hands to request for
Allah's infinite mercy
I cannot tell them he is healthier
I cannot express he is departing
For those who don't know Alzheimer's
May feel I am falsifying
My Lord You have designed my hardships
My trials are so custom made by His Majesty
He has given me the patience and strength to face it
He has helped me manage all the challenges

I beg you, my Lord, with strong faith and
spirituality
Accept all his (Qayum's) good deeds & charity

Protect my husband from severity
Please, Allah, let him have Your boundless mercy
You have reversed him to old age
You have said in the Holy book
That he will not know
After having had knowledge a thing indeed
Allah is All-Knowing and Competent (17:23)
Thank you for all your miracles
Thank you for people I have met on this journey
Thank you for taking care of me and my ,family
I beg you Allah for your infinite mercy.

Atiya Saithna (7th Jan 2022)

Alhamdulillah, even as Qayum's health faded, he adjusted well to the routines of his new carers. Their calm voices and the tranquillity of his surroundings seemed to soothe him, and for a while, I, too, found some solace in the knowledge that he was eating well and being cared for tenderly. Though his words were increasingly lost to the disease, he would still attempt to respond to my salaams—his lips moving, a bond between us that needed no translation. He would sleep more or lay in bed quietly, staring at the TV, lost in a world of his own.

In January 2022, our daughter, Amber, came to visit after travel restrictions were eased. Though her father no longer recognised her by name, she felt a connection, and perhaps—just perhaps—he did too. It was heartbreaking to witness, but she, like me, understood it was the disease, the changes in his brain, that made her a stranger to him. Yet, she stayed strong, managing the visit with grace, filled with love and compassion. Qayum's body, weakened by the relentless grip of Alzheimer's, began to betray him. His legs lost their strength, and each movement was accompanied by pain. So, I began to massage his legs with essential oils, a small comfort in his world of silent suffering. The simple touch eased his pain, allowing him to drift off to sleep. But as time passed, I saw him slipping away, day by day, into a place I could not follow any more.

Then came the news I dreaded—a urine infection sent him to the hospital. I was furious; all he needed was antibiotics. He was so frail, so unaware of his surroundings. I feared the journey to the hospital would only weaken him further. Six hours later, the hospital discharged him with a simple course of antibiotics. When I arrived the next morning, I was met with a red sign on his door that read "STOP"—he had tested positive for COVID-19.

Bless my Qayum, isolated in his room for ten days, with only carers attending to him. I stood at a distance, offering my salaams, but he looked so fragile, so distant. By Allah's mercy, he survived COVID, but I knew it had taken its toll. His body was too weak to recover fully. Soon after, the decision was made to keep him in bed, as he could no longer sit upright in his wheelchair. His decline was becoming increasingly apparent, and I knew the time was drawing near.

Palliative care was initiated. I remained strong, making calls to funeral directors, keeping our children informed, and preparing myself for what was to come. I remember clearly when Qayum refused to eat or drink. It was then that I gently dampened his lips with zam zam water, hoping to ease his discomfort. The sacred water, a gift from Allah, was the only thing I could offer him now.

I held his hand, reciting softly, knowing that even in his frail state, my touch and voice could bring him peace. I had read that touch comforts, reduces pain, and eases anxiety. I prayed it was true. Qayum's response, though slight, was there. He could still feel me.

It was Wednesday, the 25th of May 2022, two years to the day since his hip fracture, that I felt it—the presence of the angels. I texted our children, "Your dad is leaving us. He is embarking on his final journey. I can feel the angels in the room." Our daughter booked her flight immediately, arriving the morning of his death, just hours too late. But Allah had His reasons; there is wisdom in all His plans.

"And they planned and Allah (also) planned and Allah is the Best of Planners."

(Quran 3:54)

As Thursday approached, Qayum became more restless. I spent the day by his side, reciting the Quran, Surah Yaseen, and every prayer I knew that might comfort his departing soul.

I held his hands, kissed his forehead, and told him that the angels were ready to welcome him that his journey here was coming to an end, and soon he would meet Allah, his parents, his son Imran, and all those he loved. I promised him I would strive to join him in Jannah, and I thanked him—for everything, for loving me, for taking care of me, for shaping me into the woman I had become.

With trembling lips, he recited the Shahada:

"Ash-hadu an la ilaha illa-Allah wa ash-hadu anna Muhammadan rasul-Allah."

Then, with one final nod of assurance, he closed his eyes.

Alhamdulillah, his heart stopped, his soul returned to Allah, and on Friday, the 27th of May 2022—his favourite day of the week—Abdul Qayum left this world peaceful, serene, and wrapped in Allah's mercy.

Alhamdulillah, I am overwhelmed with gratitude for the greatest reward from my Creator, a reward I never imagined possible. Allah, in His infinite wisdom, heard my cries, witnessed my sleepless nights, saw my tears, my pleading, and my doubts— and granted me exactly what my heart longed for. Through His boundless mercy, He gave both Qayum and me a miraculous, divine ending. I never expected Qayum to respond as I spoke to him of meeting his Lord, yet Allah, my Rabb, showed me the ultimate truth: that trusting in Him, and Him alone, is all we ever need.

As the finality of this journey unfolded, a profound relief washed over me, and my heart swelled with gratitude. The burden that had once weighed so heavily on my soul lifted, and I thanked Allah with every fibre of my being. For days, weeks, months, and now years, I remain in awe of His care, His mercy, and His guidance throughout our journey with Alzheimer's. It was as if every moment had been divinely orchestrated—the puzzle of Qayum's life and death perfectly assembled by the hands of our Creator. Allah gave me countless opportunities to be there for Qayum in his final moments, a gift beyond measure.

Now, as I reach the end of this book, I can only reflect on the emotional terrain we've navigated together. I bow to Allah in gratitude, though no amount of prostration could ever repay His kindness, for He is Ar-Rahman, Ar-Raheem. My hope is in His infinite mercy, and I pray for forgiveness for my shortcomings. Ya Allah, please continue to take care of my family, grant us strong Eemaan, and allow us to live by the Qur'an and the Sunnah.

Bless us with the best in this life and the hereafter. Ameen.

Allah planned our trials and our storms and, in His mercy, gave us the strength to endure. We prostrated, we pleaded, and in the end, He rewarded us for persevering through one of life's most painful challenges—Alzheimer's. Alhamdulillah.

CHAPTER THIRTEEN

A LIFE OF GRATITUDE

In Honour of My Husband, Abdul Qayum

Alzheimer's took you away from me, but you left this world on a Friday, the most blessed day of Jumu'ah, to meet your Creator. For eight years, we faced unimaginable trials. I shed countless tears and faced my deepest fears, but I was always by your side. You were my rock, my pillar, my roof, the strength that held me up. I loved you more deeply than words could express, and it was this love that carried me through the darkest days of your illness.

Watching you slip away, day by day, was a heart-wrenching ordeal. Yet, you never complained, never showed impatience. It was I who wavered, who struggled to hold onto my Eemaan and my sanity. I prayed for you constantly, hoping for a miracle, for relief, for understanding.

But Allah, in His mercy, blessed us with something far greater—our children, who cared for you with unwavering devotion. The visits, the calls, and the small gestures of love were blessings we will never forget.

To this day, I cannot fully comprehend what you went through. My mind still reels, my eyes still fill with tears, and my body remembers the pain of watching you fade. But in the midst of it all, we placed our trust in Allah, and He never let us down.

In those final moments, as I recited the Qur'an by your side, I witnessed the angels of death take your hand, gently guiding you to the other side. You could not speak, but your eyelids fluttered as you affirmed, La ilaha illallah. It was the most profound affirmation of faith.

I will always miss you, but I find peace knowing you are now in the care of Allah, resting until we meet again in Jannah, our Final Abode, Insha Allah!

Half a Century

As I sit here, full of gratitude and patience, reflecting on fifty-three years of life in the UK, I cannot help but marvel at how quickly the years have passed. It feels like it was only yesterday that our journey began, and now, in the blink of an eye, so much has changed. The year 2022 was full of both love and loss, trials and triumphs. Allah took care of us through it all, reminding me constantly of His mercy.

This past year, I experienced the devastating loss of Abdul Qayum, and a few years prior, I lost Imran, my parents, the greatest loves in my life. The pain is indescribable, but Allah, in His wisdom, gave me the strength to endure. He gave me the gift of *sabr*, and I am forever grateful.

Were there early signs? I look back now, wondering if we missed something. Qayum never forgot a thing—except birthdays, perhaps. But then, slowly, changes crept in. It wasn't until he was diagnosed in 2014, much, much later, that I saw the pattern—the slow, insidious onset of Alzheimer's. He became more withdrawn and more isolated, but I attributed it to his health. I blamed his reluctance to socialise with his tiredness and his frustrations with the stresses of everyday life. I wandered through endless websites, looking for answers no doctor could give. It was a lonely journey, trying to piece together the puzzle. But in the end, we had no control. Allah had already written our path.

When did it all begin? Was his reckless driving and sudden bursts of road rage the first signs of things to come? At the time, I saw them as quirks—frustrating, yes, but nothing more than a part of who he was. Or did it start later, when he began repeating the same stories—how he arrived in the UK, where he lived, how he supported his family—as if clinging to memories that were slowly slipping away?

Could it have started when he preferred the solitude of our exquisite garden, refusing to visit friends on weekends? I convinced myself it was exhaustion, stubbornness even. But deep down, it unsettled me. It wasn't normal.

The slow retreat from social life, and the deaths in the family. Was it triggered by his angina or glaucoma surgery?

My mind spirals through all these moments, searching for answers where there are none. There was that disorienting trip to Mecca, or was it Malaysia? Spain? So many everyday complications we simply endured, unaware of what lay ahead. That's the cruel truth of Alzheimer's—you are left to piece together fragments, to seek terrifying answers online, all while no doctor dares say the words. I found solace in research, but it was a hollow comfort. I saw the symptoms but always had something else to blame.

Why didn't we notice sooner? The signs had been there for years, hidden in plain sight, but we didn't know what we were looking for. According to the Alzheimer's Society, the early symptoms are subtle and easily misinterpreted—until it's too late.

Alzheimer's disease begins long before any symptoms become apparent. This stage is called preclinical Alzheimer's disease. It's usually identified only in research settings. You and those around you won't notice symptoms during this stage.

This stage of Alzheimer's can last for years, possibly even decades. Although you won't notice any changes, new imaging technologies of the brain can identify amyloid plaques and neurofibrillary tangles. The tangles develop when tau proteins change shape and organise into structures. These are hallmarks of Alzheimer's disease.

The ability to identify these early changes is especially important for clinical trials. Ongoing trials are looking at whether treating people with preclinical Alzheimer's may delay or slow the onset of symptoms. The imaging technologies also are important as new treatments are developed for Alzheimer's disease.

Additional biomarkers have been identified for Alzheimer's disease. These are found in blood samples and can indicate an increased risk of disease. These biomarkers can be used to support the diagnosis of Alzheimer's disease, typically after symptoms appear.

Genetic tests also can tell you if you have a higher risk of Alzheimer's disease, particularly early-onset Alzheimer's disease. These tests aren't recommended for everyone. You and your healthcare provider can discuss whether genetic testing might be helpful for you.

Newer imaging techniques, biomarkers and genetic tests will become more important as new treatments for Alzheimer's disease are developed.

Qayum started withdrawing after his heart troubles, and I attributed it to his health. His moods changed, and his personality shifted, but confusion never set in, not at first. On reflection, he was easily upset at home, but how could anyone know that these small things pointed to something far more sinister—a disease that would steal him away, piece by piece?

And then there was the sugar. His love for it baffled me. Research points to many questions, and it suggests that changes in the brain might begin decades before dementia shows its face. But by then, it was too late.

Some of the changes that occur in Alzheimer's disease bear an unsettling resemblance to those found in diabetes. In both conditions, the brain's nerve cells can become resistant to insulin, a crucial hormone for processing glucose and maintaining healthy cell function. As the brain becomes deprived of the fuel it needs, the damage accumulates silently. Amyloid plaques and tau proteins begin to build up, tangling themselves within the delicate fabric of the brain. These changes slowly but relentlessly erode the person you once knew, piece by piece. It's for this reason that Alzheimer's is sometimes unofficially referred to as "Type 3 diabetes"—a disease that strikes at the core of memory, cognition, and personality in ways that still leave so much unknown.

Reflecting on our journey together, I now understand that many of the misunderstandings, the moments of distance, that arose between us as a family were not solely ours. They were shadows cast by this disease, creeping into our lives when and where only Allah knows. These tensions weren't a failure of our love but an uninvited consequence of a condition we didn't yet understand.

Alzheimer's took hold of Qayum slowly, like a storm gathering on the horizon long before it made itself known. And when I think back on our silent disagreements, I see them now through the lens of this illness. I realise they were not truly ours, but part of the fog spread over our lives, blurring the clarity of our love and our intentions.

May Allah, in His infinite mercy, forgive us both for the moments we couldn't navigate as we once did, for the words that might have hurt and for the struggles that came with the disease we could neither foresee nor control? Our hearts were always united, even when the disease tried to cast its worst shadow between us.

Through it all, I pray for forgiveness, knowing that our love remained strong and intact beneath the surface of it all, and I trust that in the eyes of our Creator, He sees the purity of our intentions despite the trials we faced. May Allah grant us both peace in this life and the next, for only He truly knows the depths of our journey.

It is my sincere hope that the Alzheimer's Society and Dementia UK will one day find a cure so the world can be free from the grip of this heartbreaking disease. December 2024 marked a new horizon of hope. In a major breakthrough for the treatment of early-stage Alzheimer's, the Medicines and Healthcare products Regulatory Agency (MHRA) approved two drugs—Lecanemab and Donanemab—as safe and effective. This step forward offers real promise and renewed optimism for families affected by this devastating condition.

Through it all, Allah has been my strength. I trust in Him fully, and I thank Him for giving me a new life after sepsis, a week after Qayum's passing. Only He knows the reason why I survived that moment, and for that, I am grateful. To every carer of an Alzheimer's patient: listen to your body and take care of your heart and soul because you, too, are on this journey with your loved one.

Alzheimer's left me with a trail of unexpected gifts and hard-won lessons. It taught me to be more self-aware, more humble, and deeply respectful of the person living with dementia. While Alzheimer's stole Qayum's abilities and capabilities, it never took away our love or our bond. I can now honour his past with a sense of peace—where challenges turned into possibilities, problems became solutions, and isolation blossomed into connections. I am full, I am complete. I saw Allah's mercy enveloping us. Together, we created new memories and forged new relationships to cherish forever.

Looking back, those moments of connection—whether in joy or in sorrow—during Qayum's long decline were worth everything to me. They offered me a chance to stay close to my husband, to see him through, even as the disease took so much. I have photos, videos, and voice memos to remind me of those precious times, and while I wish we hadn't gone through this, I feel blessed to have drawn closer to my Creator.

One quote sums up my thoughts on gratitude, a sentiment that has changed my life:

> *"Gratitude unlocks the fullness of life. It turns what we have into enough, and more. It turns denial into acceptance, chaos to order, confusion to clarity. It can turn a meal into a feast, a house into a home, a stranger into a friend."*
> *Melody Beattie*

"Gratitude" has become my daily practice. Morning and night, I give thanks—Alhamdulillah—for the opportunity to complete this book and for the blessings along the way. I am deeply thankful to my parents, Abdul Majid and Fatima, to my father for valuing my education when, at times, he could not afford my fees and to my mother for raising me with a deep love of Allah and for imparting all her talented skills. And I thank Allah for my recovery from sepsis, for without a sound mind and body, this journey would not have been possible. I thank Allah SWT for blessing me with the best of this world, and I hope for the best in the next, my Final Abode.

ABOUT THE AUTHOR

Atiya Saithna was born in Mumbai, India in 1949, grew up in Chittagong, now known as Bangladesh, completed school and college in Karachi before settling in the UK. She has dedicated her life to education, faith, and family. She has been fulfilling her father's vision which he mentions to her in a letter in 1973. His words were: "The greatest pleasure of my life would be to see my children and grandchildren on the right path—in the service of mankind at large. We must understand and fulfil the purpose of life—the purpose for which God created us—to serve Him and Humanity."

After qualifying as a teacher in 1987, she went on to serve in schools in London, eventually becoming a headteacher at an Islamic school. Her career spanned over three decades, marked by a passion for nurturing young minds and breaking barriers in faith-based education. Now retired from formal teaching, she reflects on a life shaped by migration, motherhood, and the deeply personal journey of caring for a husband with Alzheimer's.

Atiya still has the passion to teach so she has gone into volunteering roles of different kinds and she loves it, her favourite is mentoring trainee teachers with Buckingham University. She falls well into the roles given to her from admin work at Harrow Talking Newspaper for the blind to volunteering at Soul Kitchen; she loves to help the most vulnerable who come across her pathway. Allah SWT has blessed her with time to help others, may He accept it.

LETTER FROM MY FATHER

6th May 1973

Dear Ati,

I have been reading your various letters with great interest and pleasure. I am particularly very happy to learn that you have kept up reading Quran and attending to various domestic duties with real zeal, love, and fervour. Work is worship and you have learnt the real meaning and pleasure of work. Your early letters during Jan & Feb had distressed me because of loneliness & boredom you experienced then. I was sad, and always prayed that you will find out ways and means of keeping yourself busy in purposeful and constructive work. Your recent letters gave me great relief. At last the boredom and loneliness was over and you are busy—busy with all sorts of work. I do not know if you can find time for reading—reading good books and "Tafhimul Quran." Do you have Urdu or English translation of Quran? Maulana Maudoodi's Tafhimul Qur'an is a great work. If you get time do devote an hour or half on its study.

The greatest pleasure of my life would be to see my children and grand-children on the right path—in the service of mankind at large. We must understand and fulfil the purpose of life—the purpose for which God created us—to serve Him & humanity. You must remember SERVICE begins at home; like charity begins at home.

You cannot serve someone else or mankind at large better by neglecting your home; husband & children come first and foremost. If you have served them according to tenets of Islam—take it as service to part of mankind. Apply all your energy, intelligence and efforts in creating a happy home and happy world will come by itself. I am proud of you that in spite of social chaos around, you have held fast to teaching of Prophet as far as possible.

If you acknowledge this, please do on separate sheet.

With love,
Your dad
Majid

6th May 1973

Dear Ali:

I have been reading your various letters to Shahla with great interest and pleasure. I am particularly very happy to learn that you have kept up reading Quran and attending to various domestic duties with real zeal, love, and fervour. Work is worship and you have learnt the real meaning and pleasure of work. Your early letters during Jan & Feb had distressed me because of loneliness & boredom you experienced then. I was sad, and always prayed that you will find out ways and means of keeping yourself busy in purposeful and constructive work. Your recent letters gave me great relief. At last the boredom and loneliness was over and you are busy — busy with all sorts of work. I do not know if you can find time for reading — reading good books and "Tafhimul Quran". Do you have Urdu or English translation of Quran? Maulana Maudoodi's "Tafhimul Quran" is a great work. If you get time do devote hour or half on its study.

The greatest pleasure of my life would be to see my children and grand-children on the right path — in the service of mankind at large. We must understand and fulfill the purpose of life — the purpose for which God created us — to serve Him & Humanity. You must remember SERVICE begins at home; like charity begins at home.

You cannot serve someone else or mankind at large better by neglecting your home; husband & children comes first and foremost. If you have served them according to tenets of Islam — take it as service to part of mankind. Apply all your energy, intelligence and efforts in creating a happy home and happy world will come by itself. I am proud of you that inspite of social chaos around, you have held fast to teachings of Prophet as far as possible.

If you acknowledge this, please do on separate sheet.

With love,
Your dear dad
Majid

PRAISE FOR THE BOOK

Beyond the Shadows of Memory is an intimate and brave memoir—a much-needed, honest and deeply relatable lived story, filled with hope, faith, and unimaginable strength. The author takes us on a personal journey through multiple losses, grief, and the emotional terrain of caregiving, while inviting us to laugh with her through the most unexpectedly hilarious moments. I cried, I laughed, I was heartbroken for her—and above all, I came away inspired and in awe of her unwavering faith, grace, and wisdom. She is an exemplary woman, and her story is a powerful testament to love, courage, and spiritual resilience. It is truly a gift to us all.

Hajera Memon
CEO Shade 7 Publishing

This deeply moving account of Atiya Saithna's journey captures vividly the joys and challenges of her married life and how her deep faith helped navigate the pain and rift that Alzheimer's creates between patients and their nearest and dearest.

With honesty and clarity, it sheds insight into the disease, as well as its impact on carers. Highlighting the incredible resilience and patience that Sister Atiya develops under extreme duress, she finds comfort in her closeness to God even as the tests pile up relentlessly.

Ultimately, this is a testament to how challenges in life enable one to increase their trust in God and evoke gratitude even in the depths of despair, offering hope and inspiration to all who face hardship.

A much-needed book, it will help bring about understanding of how communities can support those suffering with dementia and their carers.

Shaykh Haytham Tamim
Founder and Chair of Utrujj Foundation